CB078519

Pathway to Math 2

Student's Book

Glue your picture here.

Name

Richmond

Richmond

58 St Aldates
Oxford
OX1 1ST
United Kingdom

Pathway to Math Student's Book Level 2

First Edition: March 2016
Eignth Reprint: January 2023
ISBN: 978-607-06-1256-5

Pathway to Math 2 is a collaborative work, created and designed by the Department of Educational Research of Santillana. Richmond adapted the project and created an English version.

Av. Río Mixcoac No. 274, Col. Acacias,
Benito Juárez, C.P. 03240, Ciudad de México

Publisher: Justine Piekarowicz
Editorial Team: Catalina Hernández, Natalia Herrera, Duncan Jones, Jacaranda Ruiz, Milosh Trnka
Pre-Press Coordinator: Daniel Santillán
Cover Design: Lourdes Arroyo

Cover Photograph: ©THINKSTOCK: TongRo Images (TongRo Images)

Illustrations: Martín Oyarce Gallardo

Photographs: Archivo Santillana
©THINKSTOCK: iStock pp. 21, 35, 51, 69, 85, 97, 111, 121, 137, 147 (graphic-bee), 21, 35, 51, 69, 85, 97, 111, 121, 137, 147 (luctra_design).

Printed in Brazil by Forma Certa
Lote: 774583
Cod: 292712565

Introduction

Hi friends!

We are **Spot**  and **Kiki**  and we are here to welcome you to **Pathway to Math**. Follow us on the Pathway to Math, where learning becomes special. Do you want to know why?

- This pathway is full of magic, and everyone is welcome on it. You will find information, texts, pictures and activities presented in a simple and friendly manner. Here you will discover that learning is fun!
- This is a pathway where we can all learn to share and live together. The activities will help us reflect on our values and learn to respect others.

- This is a pathway open to people from all over the world where you can learn interactively with the help of the latest technology.
- This is a pathway full of challenges that involve finding solutions, developing math skills and applying calculation strategies that you and your classmates will work on together.

We will be with you every step of the way!
All you need is curiosity and the desire to learn.

How is your textbook organized?

Pathway to Math 2 is organized into five units. Here is what you will find in each unit.

Initial Pages

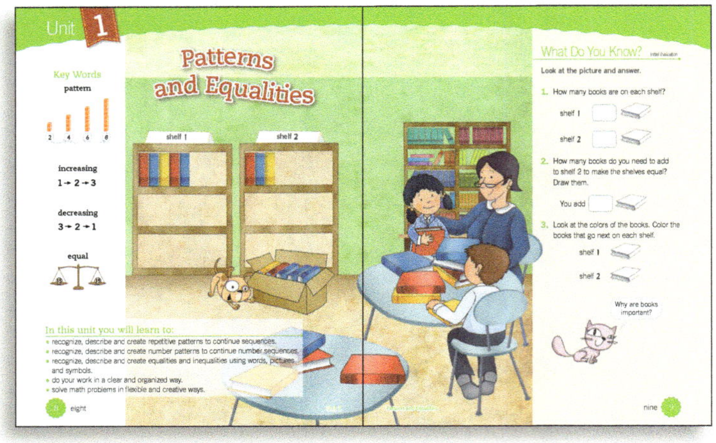

- Number and title of the unit
- Learning objectives
- Initial evaluation

Sections Organized by Learning Objectives

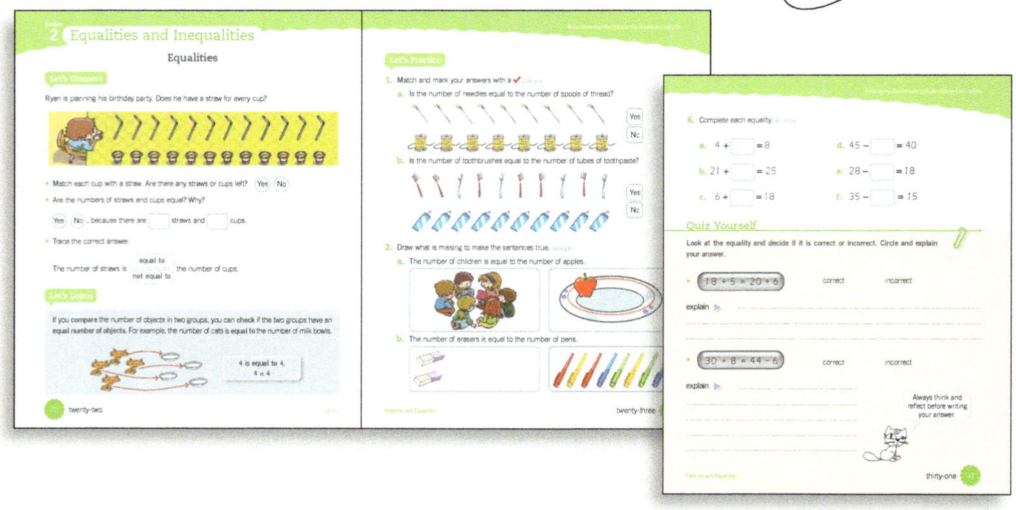

- Let's Connect
- Let's Learn
- Let's Practice
- Quiz Yourself

Fun Features

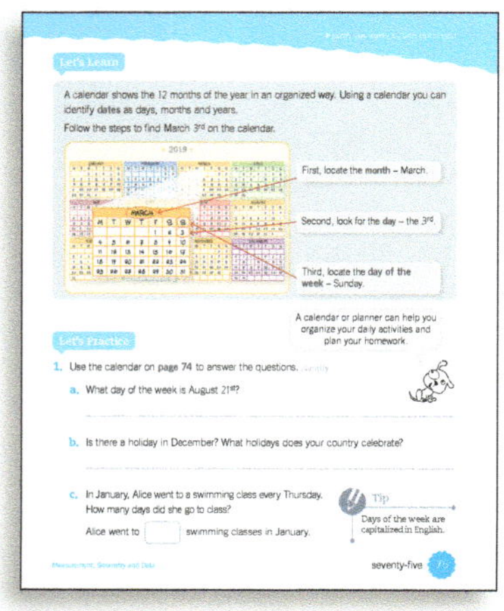

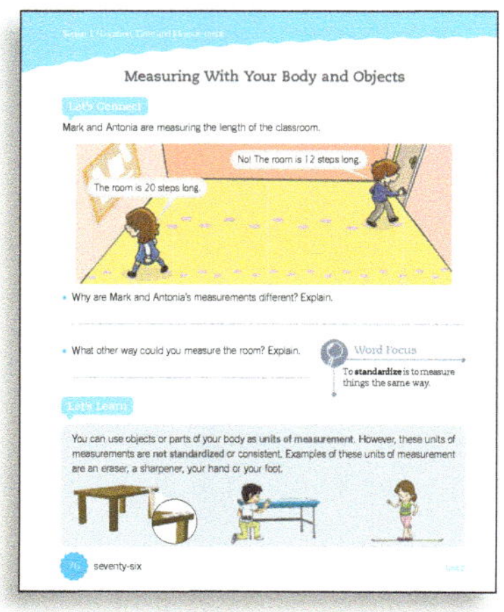

- Education through Values
- Did You Know...?
- Remember
- Tip
- Word Focus
- Fun Fact!
- Challenge

Evaluation Pages

- What Do You Know?
  Initial Evaluation
- Let's Check!
  Intermediate Evaluation
- What Did You Learn?
  Final Evaluation

Special Pages

- Exam Strategies
- Test Study Pages
  Summary and Review

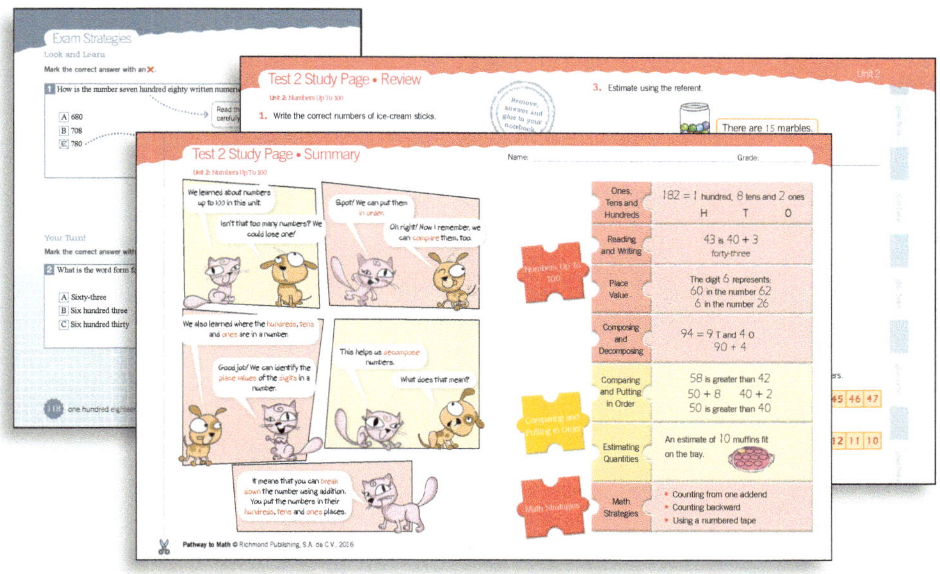

Support Pages

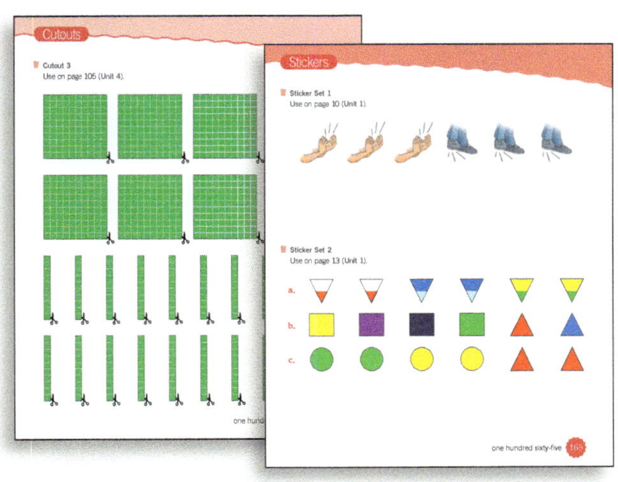

- Cutouts
- Stickers

Table of Contents

Unit 1

Patterns and Equalities

Key Words

pattern

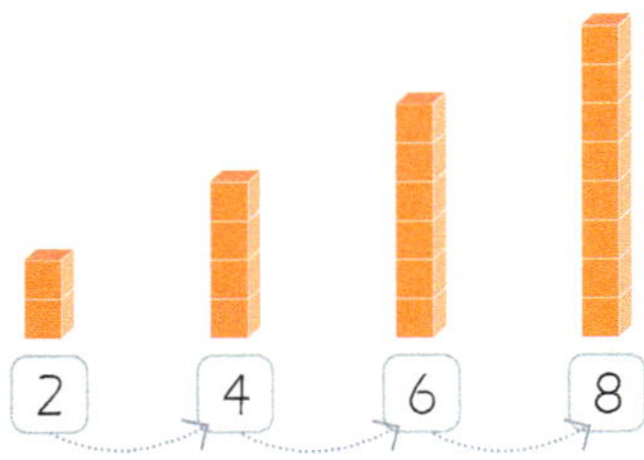

increasing

1 → 2 → 3

decreasing

3 → 2 → 1

equal

In this unit you will learn to:

- recognize, describe and create repetitive patterns to continue sequences.
- recognize, describe and create number patterns to continue number sequences.
- recognize, describe and create equalities and inequalities using words, pictures and symbols.
- do your work in a clear and organized way.
- solve math problems in flexible and creative ways.

What Do You Know? Initial Evaluation

Look at the picture and answer.

1. How many books are on each shelf?

shelf 1 ☐ 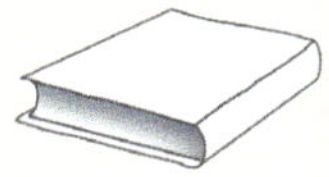

shelf 2 ☐ 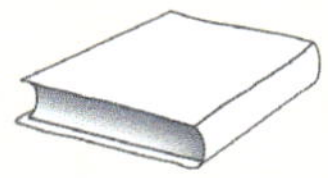

2. How many books do you need to add to shelf 2 to make the shelves equal? Draw them.

You add ☐ 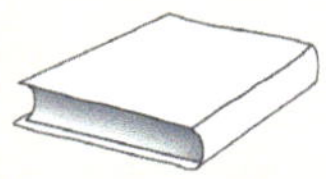

3. Look at the colors of the books. Color the books that go next on each shelf.

shelf 1 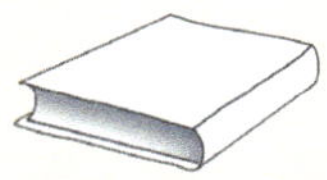

shelf 2 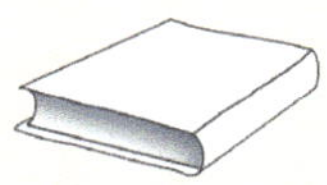

Repetitive Patterns

Let's Connect

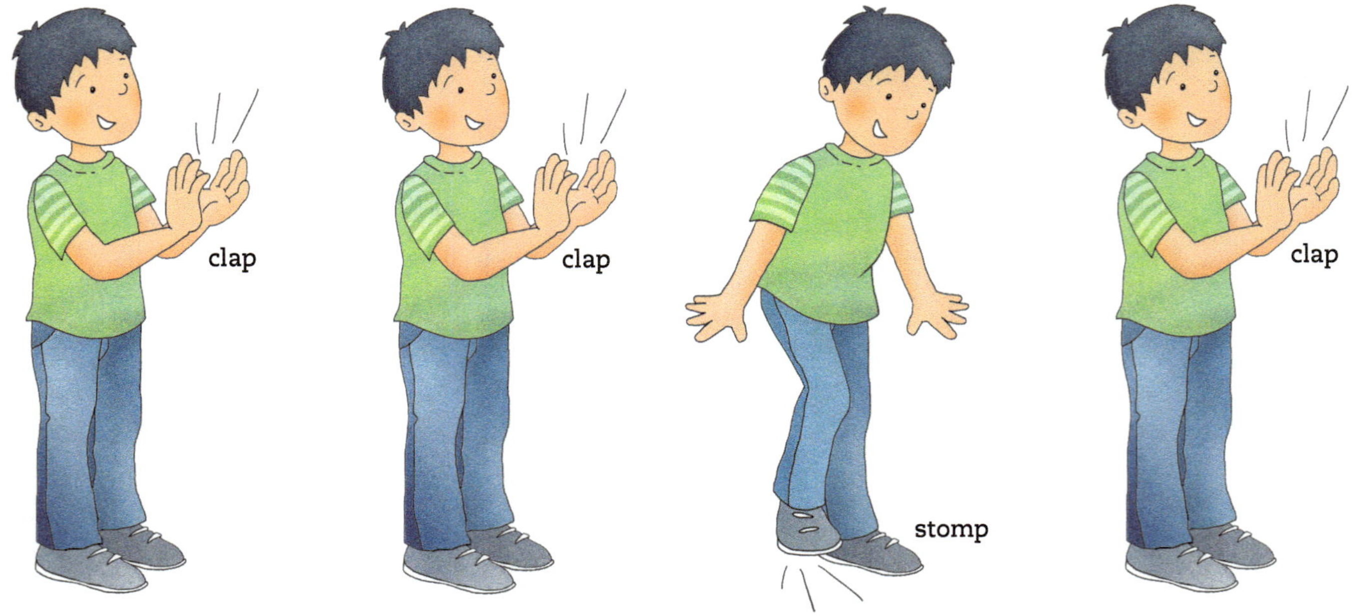

- Put Tom's claps and stomps in order using **Sticker Set 1** on **page 165.**

- How many times does Tom clap before stomping?
- How many times does Tom stomp before clapping again?
- What should Tom do after the last clap? Circle.

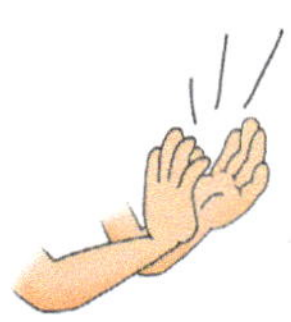

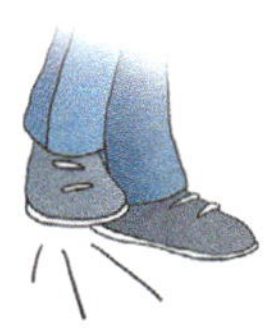

Challenge

You can use patterns to make beats and music. Can you clap and stomp a beat with your class?

Let's Learn

A **pattern** is a **rule** that makes a **sequence** of elements, shapes or sounds. It is defined by a certain characteristic, for example, color, shape or size.

pattern ▶ 2 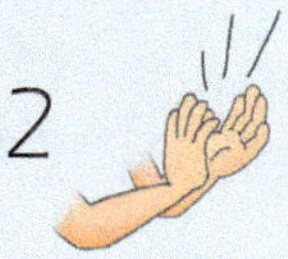 and 1 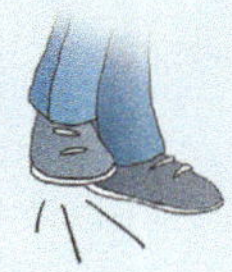

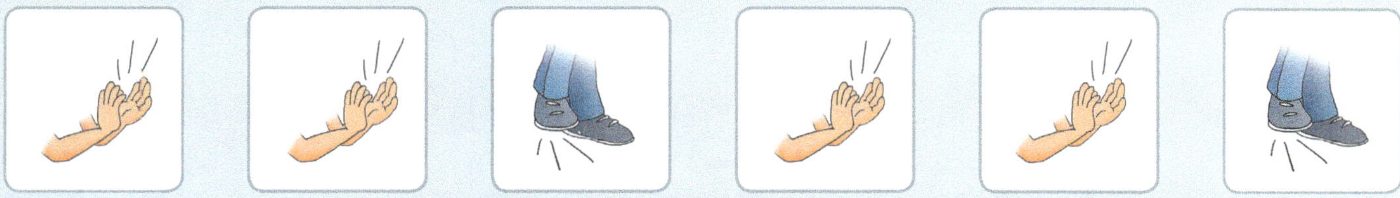

Let's Practice

1. Look at each sequence of shapes. Mark the characteristics that define each pattern with a ✓. Follow the example. Understand

___ color ✓ shape ___ size

a. 
___ color ___ shape ___ size

b. 
___ color ___ shape ___ size

c. 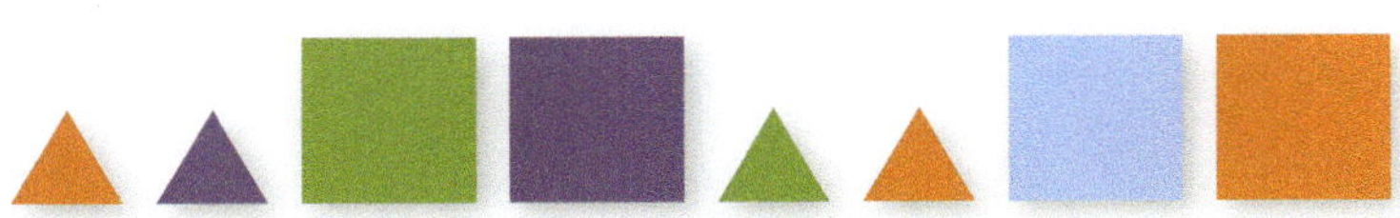
___ color ___ shape ___ size

2. Write the pattern for each sequence. Interpret

a.

pattern ▶ ____  and ____ 

b.

pattern ▶ ____ , ____  and ____ 

3. Circle the instrument that goes next in each sequence. Interpret

a.

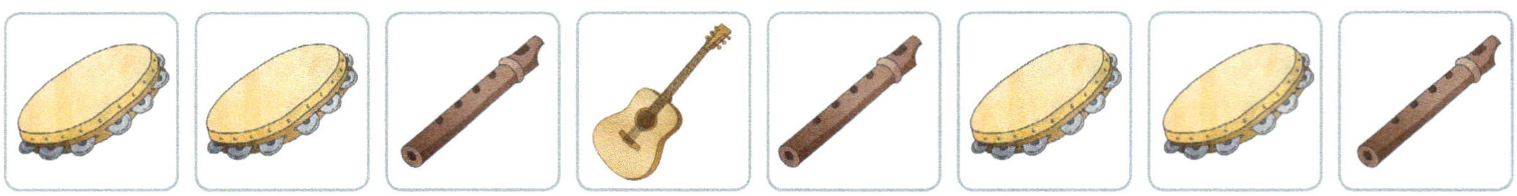

recorder

guitar

tambourine

b.

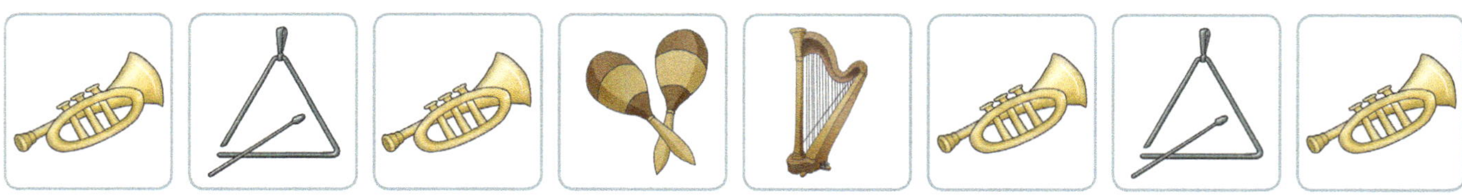

harp

trumpet

maracas

triangle

4. Continue the sequences with **Sticker Set 2** on **page 165**. Apply

a.

b.

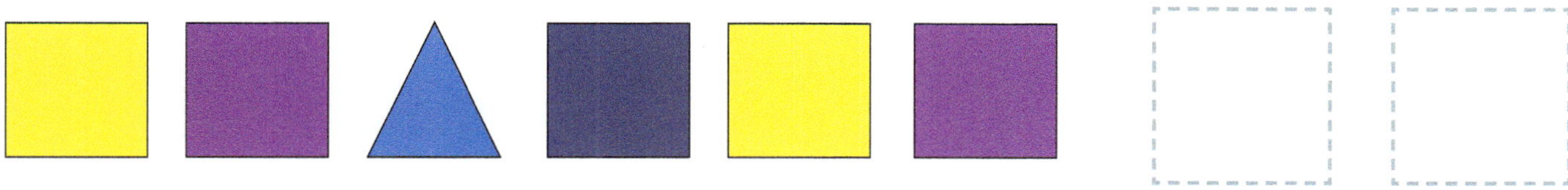

c.

5. Use **Sticker Set 3** on **page 167** to make your own patterns. Create the sequences. Create

a. pattern ▶ ____ ____ and ____ ____

b. pattern ▶ ____ ____ , ____ ____ and ____ ____

Number Patterns

Let's Connect

Claire is making a tower using blocks.

step 1 step 2 step 3 step 4

- How many blocks does each tower have?

step 1 step 2 step 3 step 4

- Does she add or remove blocks in each step? Circle.

add remove

- How many blocks did Claire add to the tower in step 2?

- How many did she add in step 3?

- Does she always add the same number of blocks? Circle.

yes no

Let's Learn

A **number pattern** is a **rule** that makes a group of ordered numbers called a **number sequence**.

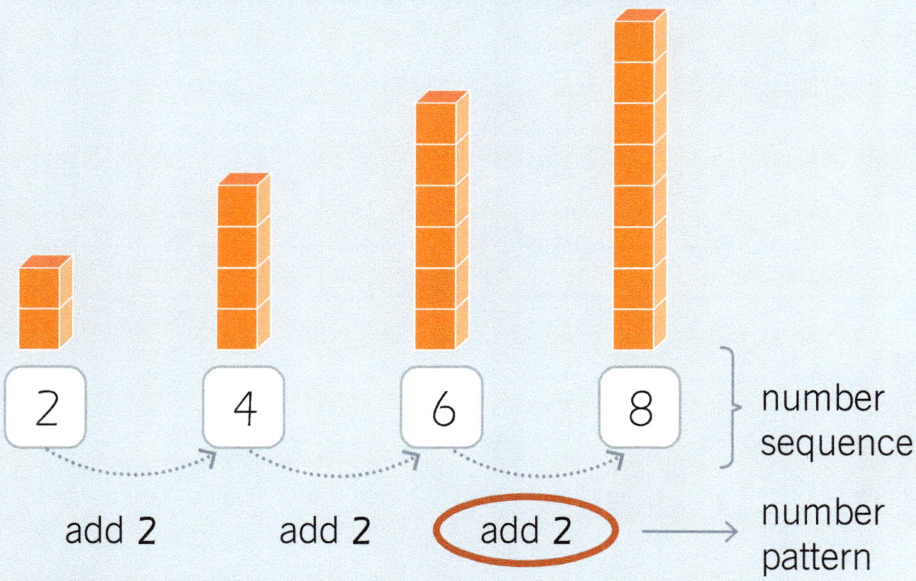

Number sequences can be:

- **Increasing** ↑, when you **add** or **sum**.
- **Decreasing** ↓, when you **remove** or **subtract**.

Did You Know...?

Number sequences are a big part of nature, too. Sea shells, flowers and other natural things all have parts that form a number sequence.

If the pattern is "add 2," you can also write it as "+ 2."

Let's Practice

1. Mark the correct pattern for each sequence with a ✔. Understand

a.

- ◯ remove 
- ◯ add 
- ◯ remove 

b.

- ◯ remove 
- ◯ add 
- ◯ add 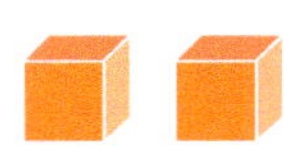

2. Identify the patterns. Continue the sequences using **Sticker Set 4** on **page 167**. Understand

a.

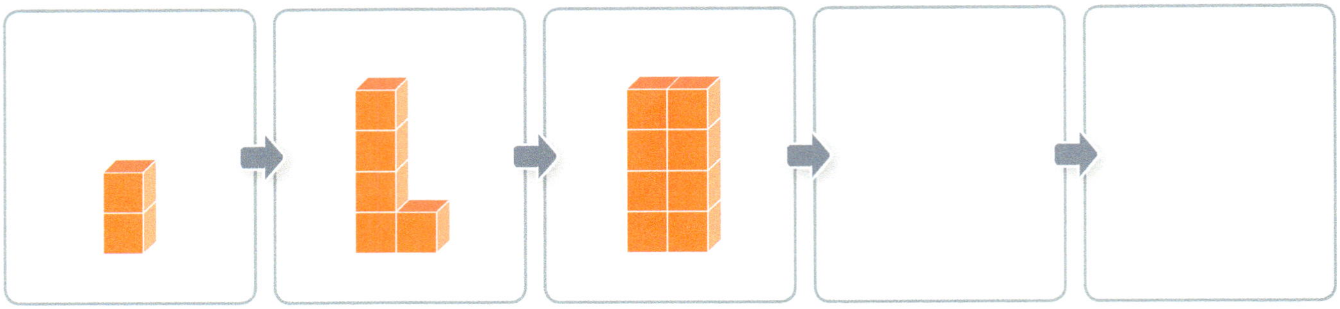

b.

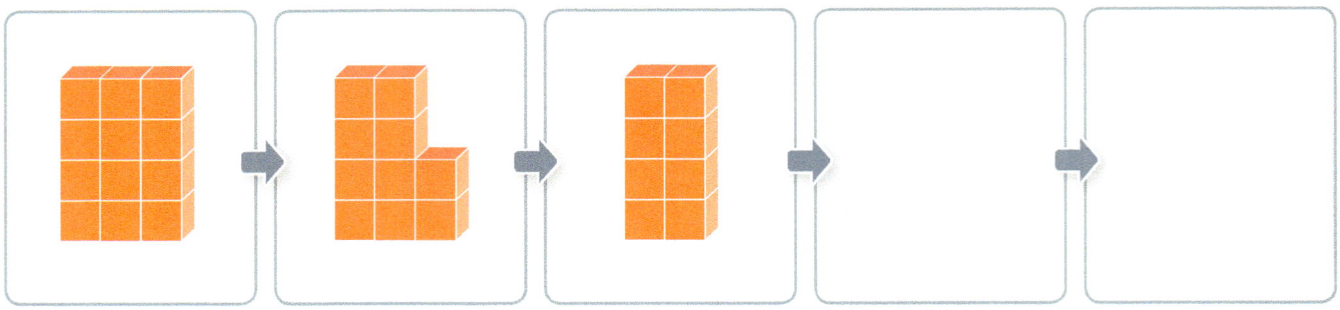

3. Continue the sequences. Circle the numbers that represent the  that go in . Analyze

a.

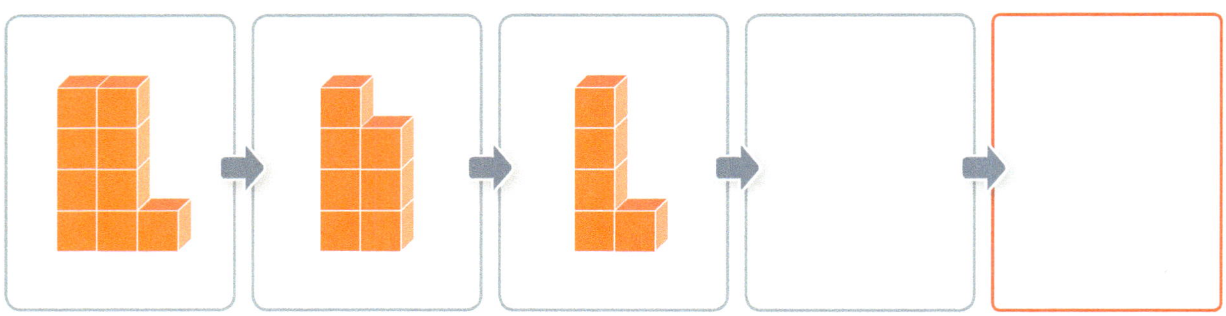

1

2

3

b.

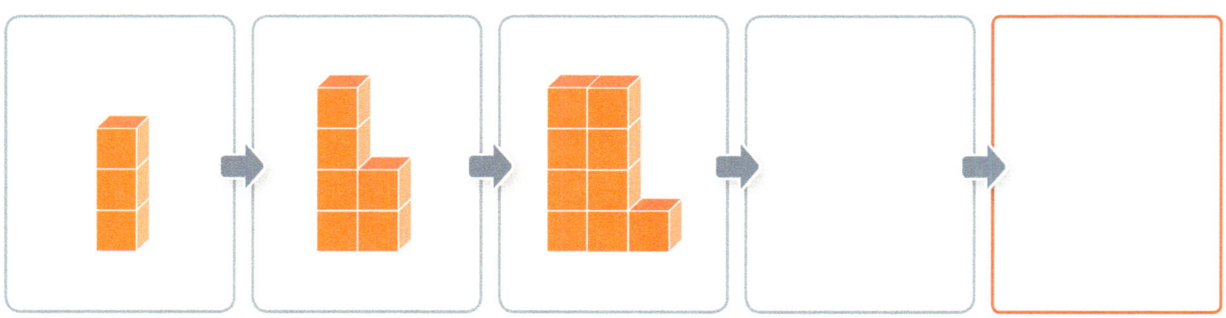

12

15

18

4. The bee wants to fly to the flower. Use an "add 3" pattern to color the path the bee should take. Apply

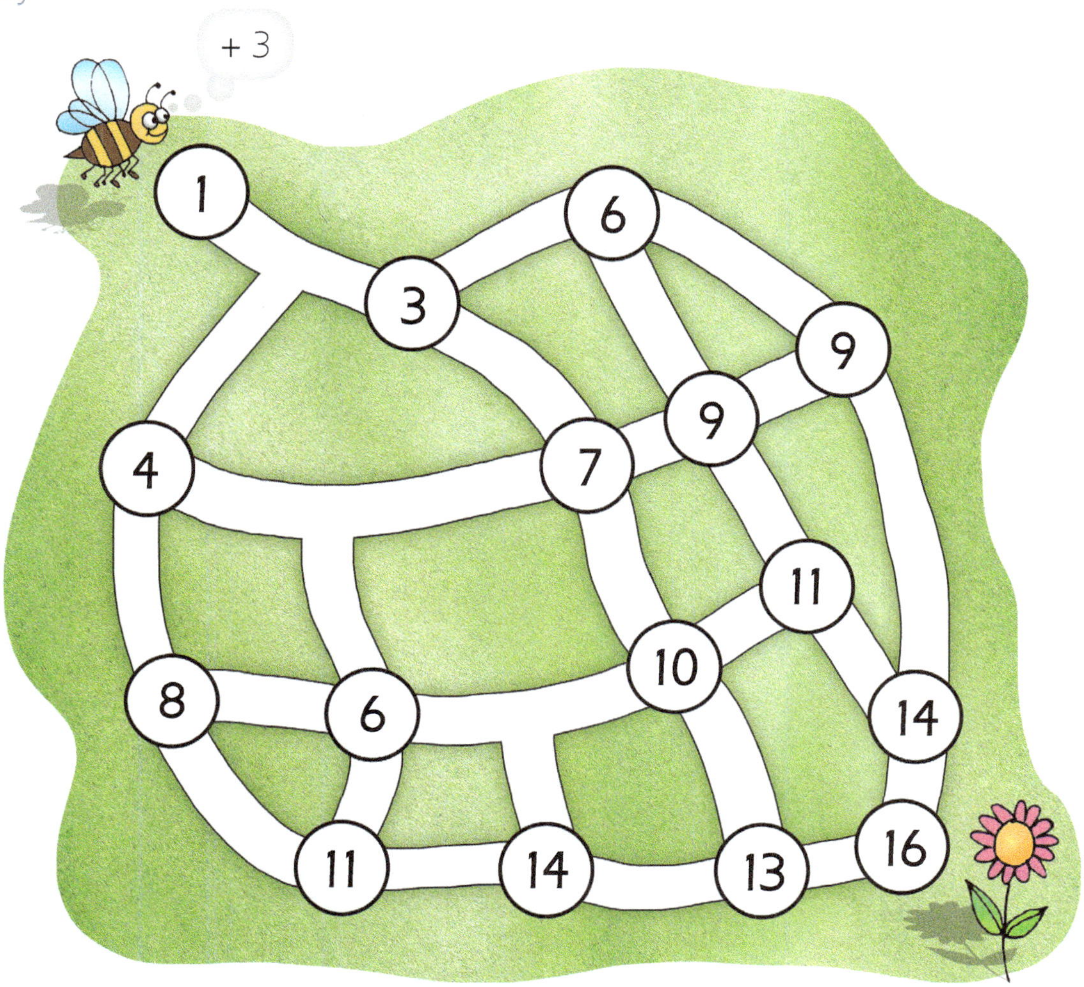

5. Circle the pattern for each sequence. Analyze

a. 1 ➡ 6 ➡ 11 ➡ 16 ➡ 21   add 3   add 5   subtract 5

b. 12 ➡ 11 ➡ 10 ➡ 9 ➡ 8   add 1   subtract 1   subtract 5

c. 22 ➡ 24 ➡ 26 ➡ 28 ➡ 30   add 2   add 3   subtract 2

6. Write the patterns and continue the number sequences. Apply

a.

1	3	5			

b.

15	12	9			

c.

38	34	30			

7. Color the number that does not fit the pattern for each number sequence. Analyze

a. 2 → 4 → 6 → 8 → 9 → 10

b. 1 → 5 → 9 → 13 → 17 → 18

c. 22 → 20 → 18 → 17 → 16 → 14

8. Create an increasing number sequence and a decreasing number sequence that follow a pattern. Start with any number. Apply

a. increasing pattern ▶ ☐

☐ → ☐ → ☐ → ☐ → ☐ → ☐

b. decreasing pattern ▶ ☐

☐ → ☐ → ☐ → ☐ → ☐ → ☐

Quiz Yourself

Look at the picture. Read the word problem and answer.

Mike follows a pattern to make a tower. He has 15 blocks to make the tower. The tower will have 5 floors. The first floor has 5 blocks and the last floor has 1 block. What pattern will Mike use to make his tower?

____

____

____

Let's Check!

Repetitive Patterns

1. Write the pattern for each sequence.

a.

☐  and ☐ 

b.

☐  and ☐ 

2. Find the patterns. Continue each shape sequence with **Sticker Set 5** on **page 169**.

a.

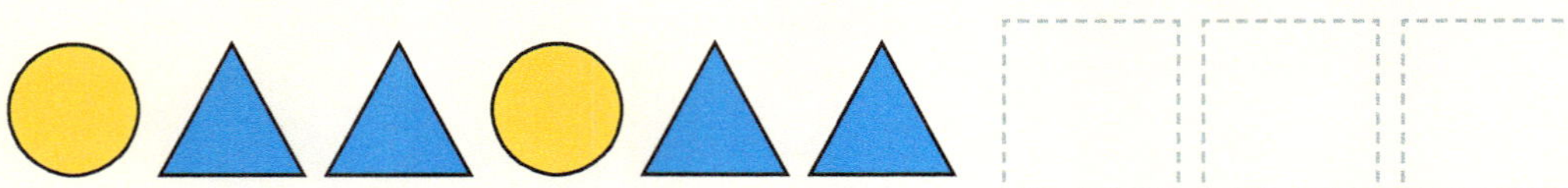

b.

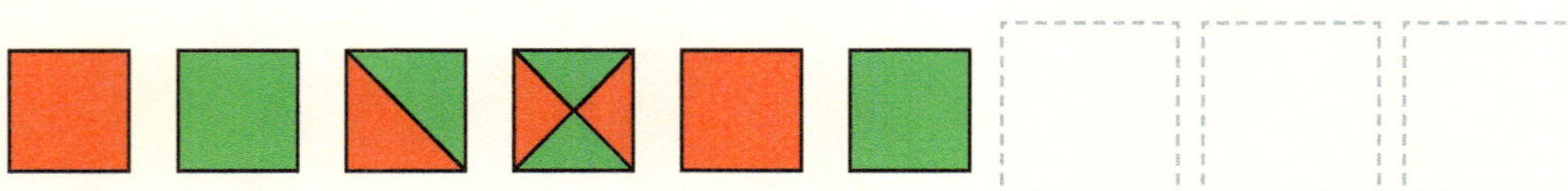

c.

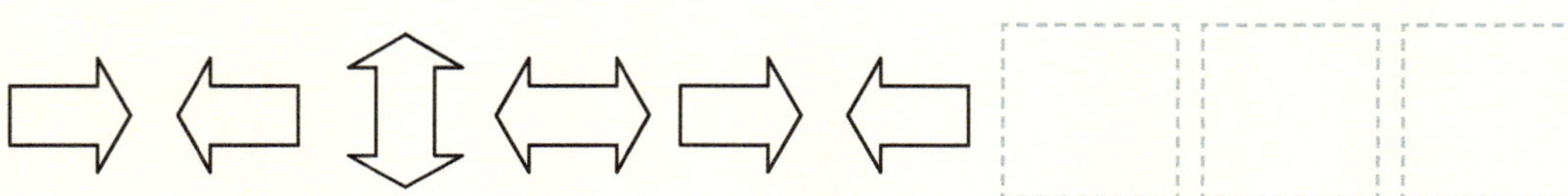

Number Patterns

3. Circle the pattern for each number sequence.

a. 14 → 12 → 10 → 8 → 6 add 1 add 2 subtract 2

b. 21 → 22 → 23 → 24 → 25 add 1 add 2 subtract 1

4. Write the patterns. Continue the number sequences.

a. ☐

7 | 10 | 13 | ☐ | ☐ | ☐

b. ☐

30 | 25 | 20 | ☐ | ☐ | ☐

How Did You Do?

For each 🐸 color a ⬭.

Section
2 Equalities and Inequalities

Equalities

Let's Connect

Ryan is planning his birthday party. Does he have a straw for every cup?

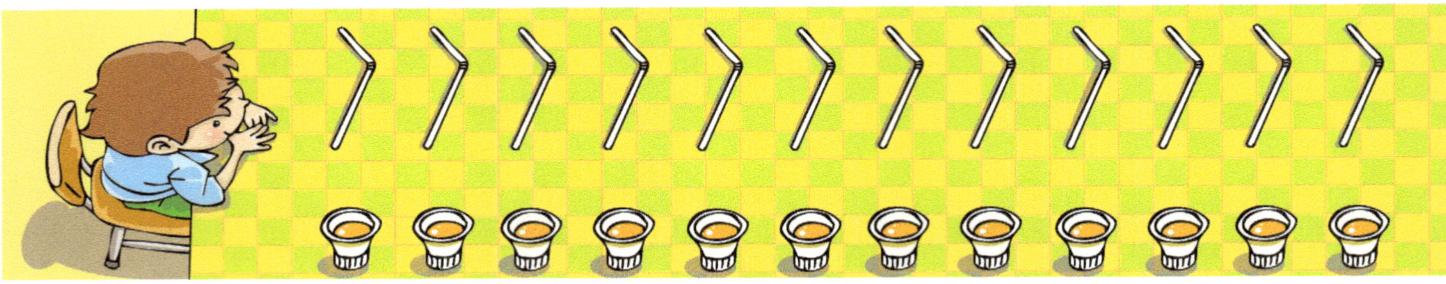

- Match each cup with a straw. Are there any straws or cups left? (Yes) (No)
- Are the numbers of straws and cups equal? Why?

(Yes) (No), because there are ☐ straws and ☐ cups.

- Trace the correct answer.

The number of straws is **equal to** / **not equal to** the number of cups.

Let's Learn

If you **compare** the number of objects in two groups, you can **check** if the two groups have an **equal number of objects**. For example, the number of cats is **equal to** the number of milk bowls.

4 is **equal to** 4.

4 = 4

Let's Practice

1. Match and mark your answers with a ✓. Apply

a. Is the number of needles equal to the number of spools of thread?

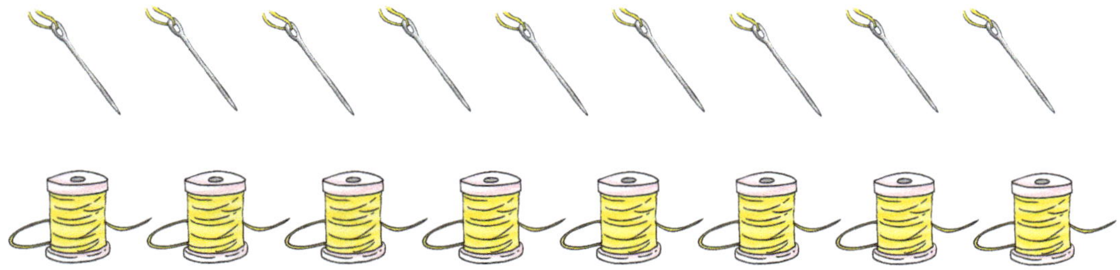

Yes

No

b. Is the number of toothbrushes equal to the number of tubes of toothpaste?

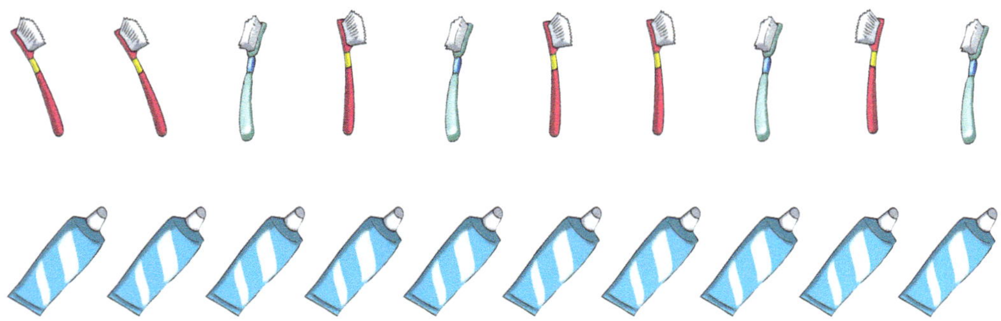

Yes

No

2. Draw what is missing to make the sentences true. Analyze

a. The number of children is equal to the number of apples.

b. The number of erasers is equal to the number of pens.

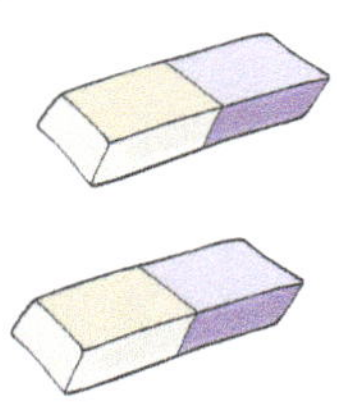

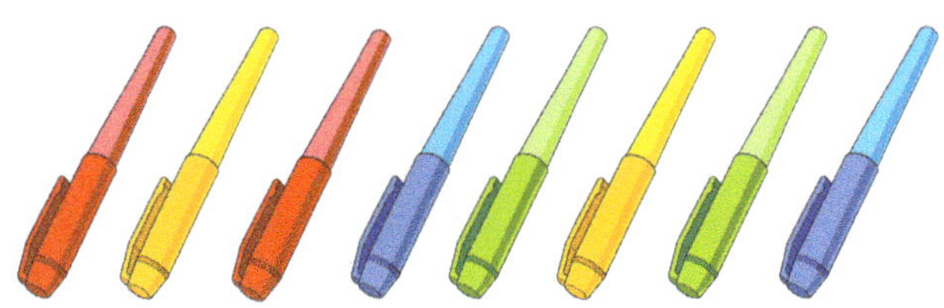

Inequalities

Let's Connect

cell phones

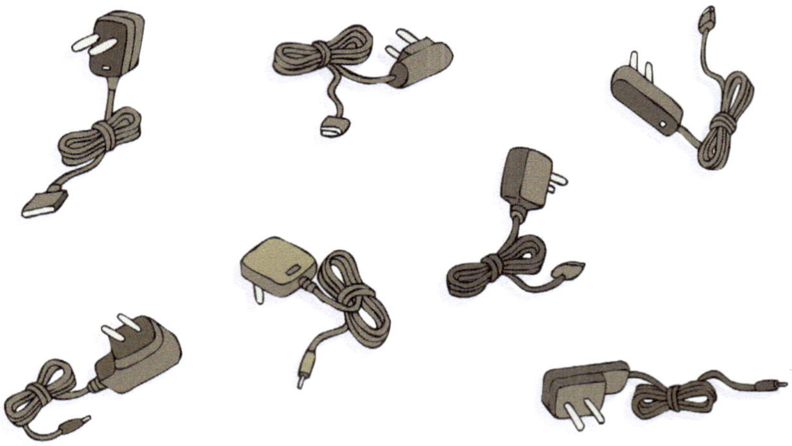

chargers

- Match each cell phone with a charger. Are there any cell phones or chargers left? Yes No
- Is the number of cell phones and chargers equal? Explain.

Yes No , because there are ☐ cell phones and ☐ chargers.

- Trace the correct answer.

The number of cell phones **is equal to** / **is not equal to** the number of chargers.

Let's Learn

Two groups **do not have an equal number of objects** if there are objects **left over** when you try to match them.

The number of dogs is **not equal to** the number of kennels.

2 is **not equal to** 4.

2 is **less than** 4.

Let's Practice

1. Compare the dice. Trace the correct answers. Apply

a. 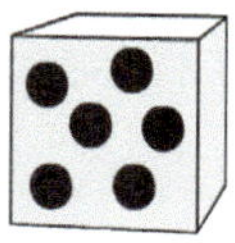 is equal to / not equal to 

b. 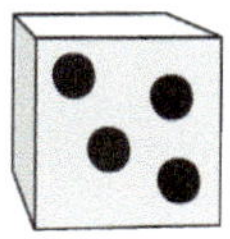 is equal to / not equal to 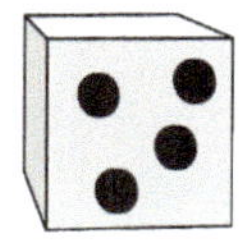

Challenge

Have your partner roll two dice and add the numbers. You now have three chances to roll your partner's number. You may choose to roll one or both of the dice each turn.

2. Draw the missing marbles to make the sentences true. Analyze

a. The number of marbles in Jar 1 is less than the number of marbles in Jar 2.

Jar 1 

Jar 2 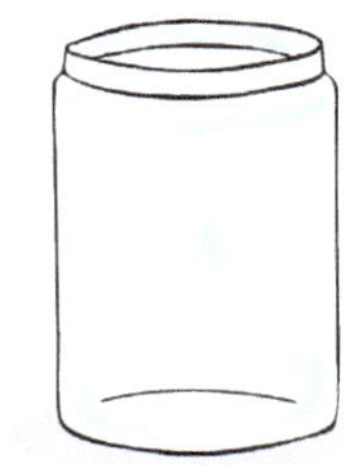

b. The number of marbles in Jar 1 is greater than the number of marbles in Jar 2.

Jar 1 

Jar 2 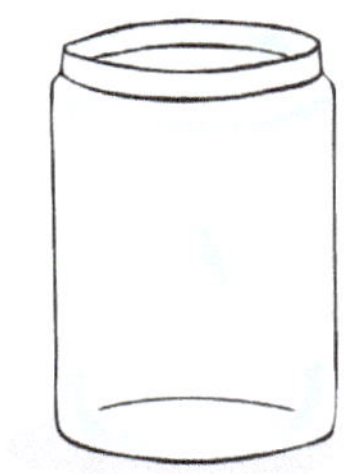

Education through Values

Recycling helps protect our planet. Remember to recycle as much as you can!

Equalities and Inequalities

Let's Connect

- How many ■ are on each of the scale's pans? Complete.

 ☐

 ☐

Fun Fact!

A **scale** is a symbol for justice and fairness, especially in courts of law. Why do you think that is?

- Which scale corresponds to the picture with the boy? Circle.

balanced

imbalanced

- Look at the picture with the boy. Why do you think the right side of the scale is lower?

____

____

- What could you do to the left side to balance the scale? And to the right side?

____

____

Let's Learn

An **equality** is a relationship between **two quantities** that are the **same**. It can be represented by a **balanced** scale.

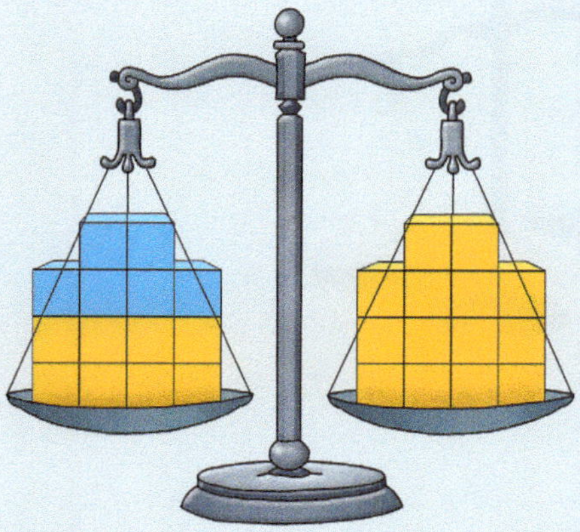

8 + 6 **is equal to** 14

$8 + 6 = 14$

$14 = 14$

An **inequality** is a relationship between **two quantities that are not the same**. It can be represented by an **imbalanced** scale.

8 **does not equal** 14

Challenge

Make a scale with a ruler and an eraser or ball. Practice balancing each side with blocks or other toys.

Education through Values

Equality is more than just a math concept. All people are **equal** and share the same rights.

Let's Practice

1. Mark the scale that represents equality with a ✔ and the scale that represents inequality with an ✘. Recognize

☐ 

☐ 

2. Use **Sticker Set 6** on **page 169** to represent balance and imbalance. Exemplify

a. 

b. 

3. Write the number of  that you need to add to the red pans to balance the scales. Analyze

a.

Add ☐ .

b.

Add ☐ .

4. Write the number of  that you need to subtract from the green pans to balance the scales. Analyze

a.

Subtract ☐ .

b.

Subtract ☐ .

5. Go to **Sticker Set 7** on **page 169**. Use the key to help you make the scales equal. Analyze

24 5 7 10

a.

___ plus ___ is equal to 15

___ + ___ = ___

b.

___ minus ___ is equal to 14

___ – ___ = ___

c.

___ minus ___ is equal to 17

___ – ___ = ___

6. Complete each equality. Analyze

a. 4 + ☐ = 8

b. 21 + ☐ = 25

c. 6 + ☐ = 18

d. 45 – ☐ = 40

e. 28 – ☐ = 18

f. 35 – ☐ = 15

Quiz Yourself

Look at the equality and decide if it is correct or incorrect. Circle and explain your answer.

- 18 + 5 = 20 + 6 correct incorrect

explain ▶ ______________________________

____

____

- 30 + 8 = 44 – 6 correct incorrect

explain ▶ ______________________________

____

____

____

____

Exam Strategies

Look and Learn

Mark the correct answer with an ✗ .

Read the instructions. They will tell you how to answer the question.

1 What is the value of ▇ to balance the scale?

The question is related to the picture. Analyze it before you answer.

☒ A 6

B 8

Look for the correct answer. Mark the answer with an ✗.

Your Turn!

Mark the correct answer with an ✗ .

2 What is the pattern of the sequence?

A Add .

B Add .

What Did You Learn?

Final Evaluation

Repetitive Patterns

1. Find the patterns. Use colored pencils to continue the sequences.

a.

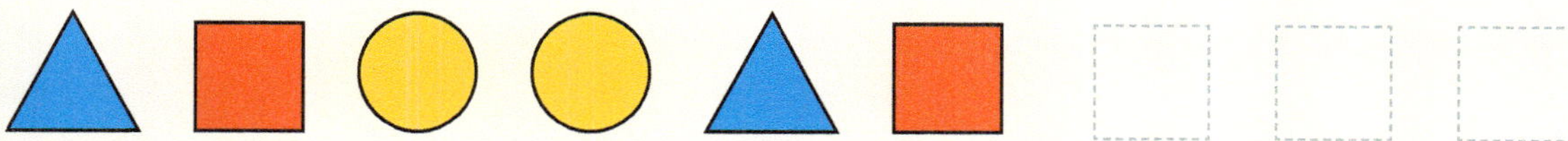

b.

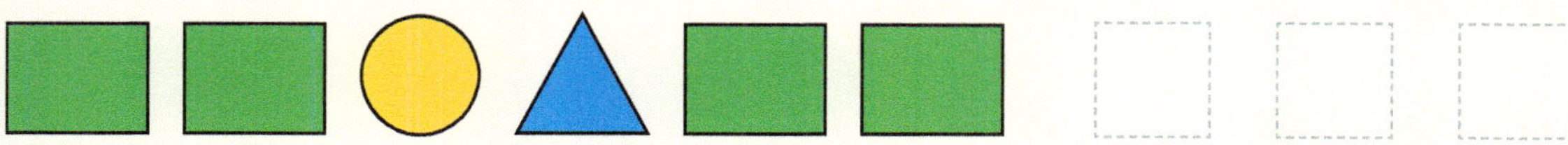

c.

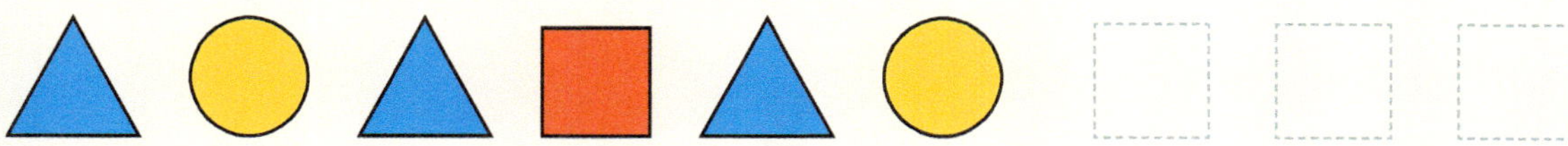

Number Patterns

2. Write the pattern for each number sequence. Continue the sequences.

a. 23 25 27 ___ ___ ___

b. 10 17 24 ___ ___ ___

c. 24 21 18 ___ ___ ___

3. Create a number sequence with a pattern.

Equalities and Inequalities

4. Draw the ● needed to balance each scale.

a.

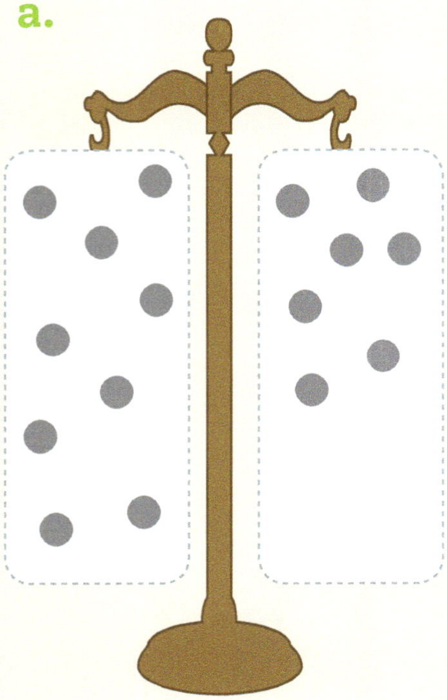

b.

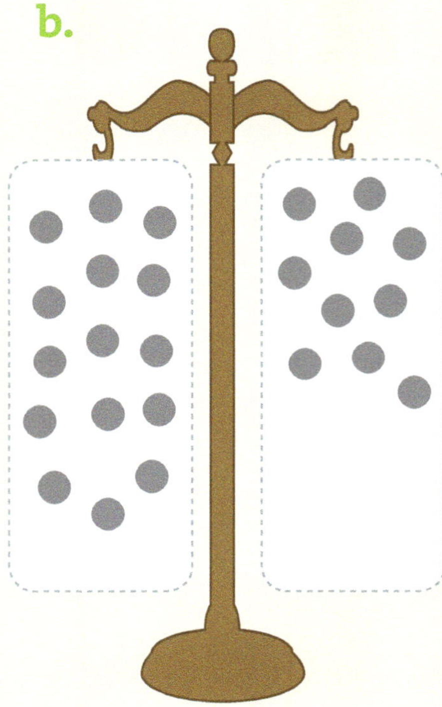

5. Write the number that balances each scale.

a.

b.

Mark the correct answer with an ✕ .

Use this number sequence to answer questions 6 and 7.

6 → 9 → 12 → 15 → 18

6. What is the pattern for the sequence?

A Add 2

B Add 3

7. Which number continues the number sequence?

A 20

B 21

8. What is the missing number in the equality?

$$33 + \square = 38$$

A 5

B 6

Find Test 1 Study Page

How Did You Do?

For each 🐸 color a ⬭.

Numbers Up To 100

Key Words

place value

ones

tens

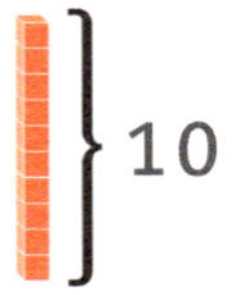

hundreds

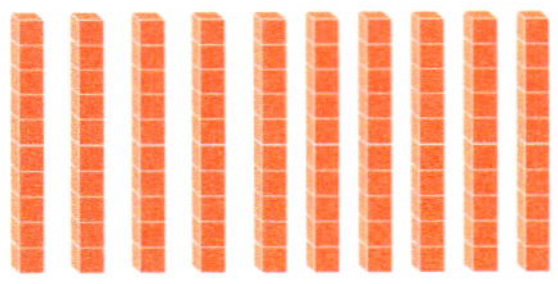

estimate

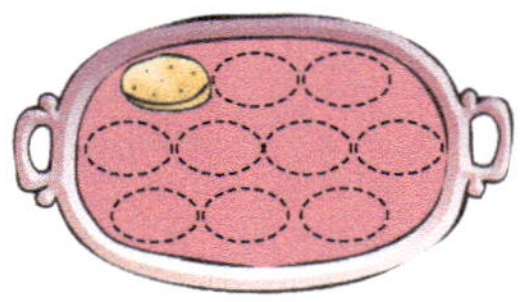

In this unit you will learn to:

- identify hundreds and the place value of digits.
- compose and decompose numbers up to 100.
- compare and put numbers up to 100 in order.
- estimate quantities up to 100 using a referent.
- count forward and backward, and use mental math strategies.

What Do You Know?

Initial Evaluation

Look at the picture and answer.

1. Write how many animals there are in the picture.

2. Which group has the most animals?

3. Use **Sticker Set 8** on **page 171.** Put the animals in order from least to most.

4. Circle the chicks in groups of 10.

5. How many tens (10s) of chicks are there?

There are ☐ tens (10s) of chicks.

Word Focus

Least means the smallest number of something, and **most** means the largest number of something.

Ones, Tens and Hundreds

Let's Connect

David is packing jars into boxes for recycling.

- How many tens (10s) and ones (1s) did David separate the 34 jars into?

☐ tens (10s) and ☐ ones (1s)

If David saves these jars in total:

- How many boxes will he need? Circle the jars in tens.

☐ boxes.

- How many jars will not be in a box?

☐ jars.

Remember!

1s are represented by 1 object and 10s are represented by 10 objects.

Let's Learn

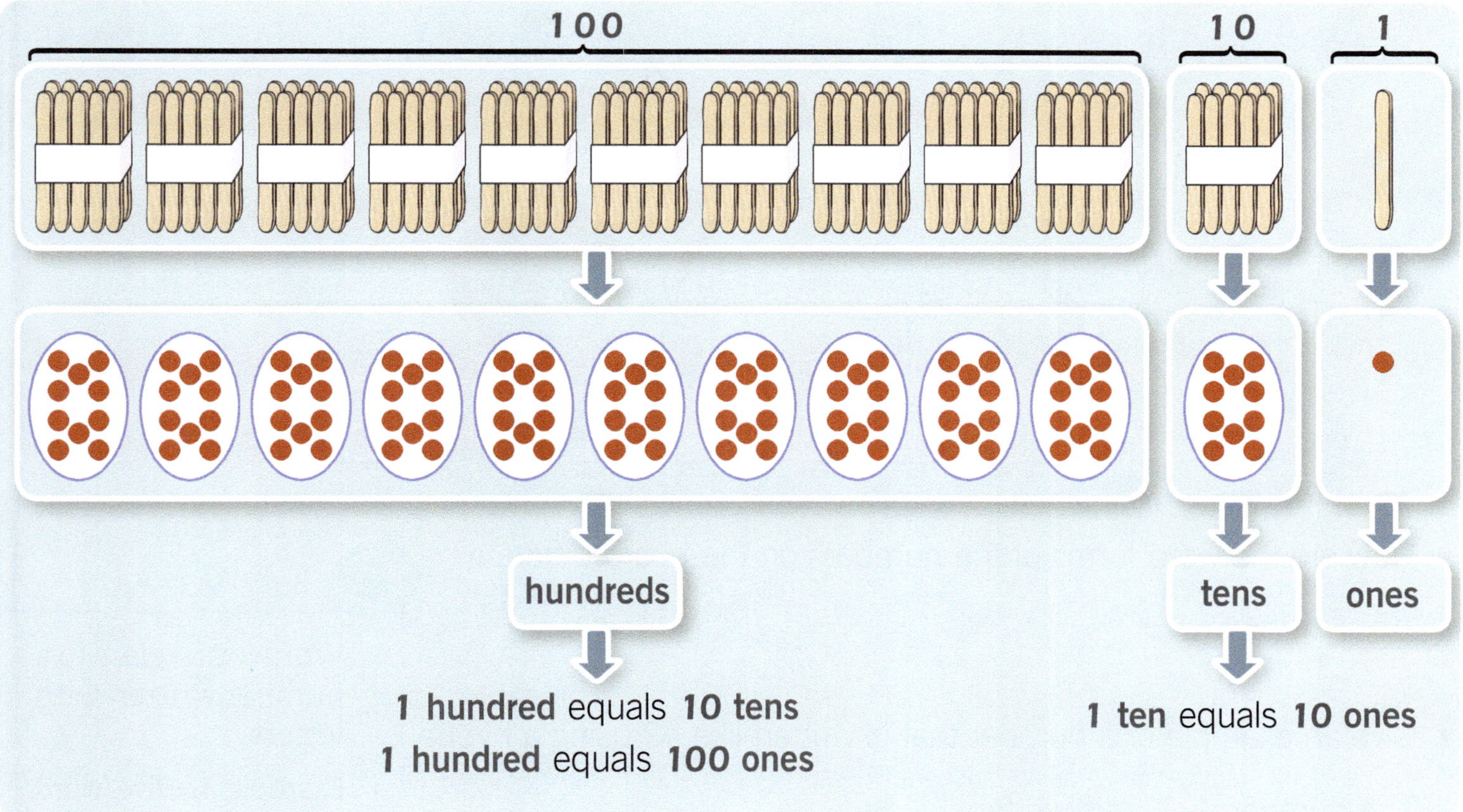

Let's Practice

1. Complete the activity. Identify

a. Color 25 ones.

b. Circle 7 tens.

Did You Know...?

Ones (O) are related to the number **one (1)**. **Tens (T)** are related to the number **ten (10)** and **hundreds (H)** are related to the number **one hundred (100)**.

Reading and Writing Numbers Up To 100

Let's Connect

- How are the word forms of the numbers on the board different?

  ____.

- Give an example of a number that is written like 42 using a hyphen.

  The number ☐ is written ______________________.

- Give an example of a number that is written like 17 using "teen."

  The number ☐ is written ______________________.

Word Focus

Word form refers to a number written with letters.

Example: 5 = five (word form)

Let's Learn

Numbers from one to twenty are written with one word.

6 ➡ six   8 ➡ eight

Numbers from 13 to 19 are written with a "teen" at the end.

14 ➡ fourteen   19 ➡ nineteen

Numbers from 21 are written using two words separated by a hyphen (-).

21 ➡ twenty-one   98 ➡ ninety-eight

Thirty, forty, fifty, sixty, seventy, eighty and ninety are exceptions.

Let's Practice

1. Match each number with its word form. Relate

a.	18	two
b.	88	eighty-eight
c.	11	eighteen
d.	2	eleven

Challenge

How old are you? Ask a classmate how old he or she is. On an index card, write his or her name and age in word form. Decorate it. Give it to your friend as a gift.

2. Match each number in word form with the correct number. Relate

a.	ten	15
b.	ninety-two	10
c.	fifteen	92

Fun Fact!

Young people between the ages of 13 and 19 are called "teenagers."

3. Write the word form for each number. Understand

a. 3 → ____________________

b. 67 → ____________________

c. 14 → ____________________

Representing Numbers According to Their Place Value

Let's Connect

Christina has lots of ice-cream sticks. She puts them in groups of 10.

- How many tens or groups of 10 did Christina make?

  She made ☐ tens, which equal ☐ ones.

- How many ones are left?

  ☐ ones are left.

- How many ice-cream sticks does Christina have?

  She has ☐ ice-cream sticks.

Remember!

Place value is the **value** a digit has according to its **position** in a number. In the number 25, for example:
2 is in the tens place = 20
5 is in the ones place = 5

- If Christina has 36 ice-cream sticks, how many groups of ten does she have? How many ones are left? Represent them using **Sticker Set 9** on **page 171**.

- Is the digit 6 in 36 and 63 represented by the same amount of ice-cream sticks? Explain.

____

____

Let's Learn

These numbers were formed using the **same digits**.

23

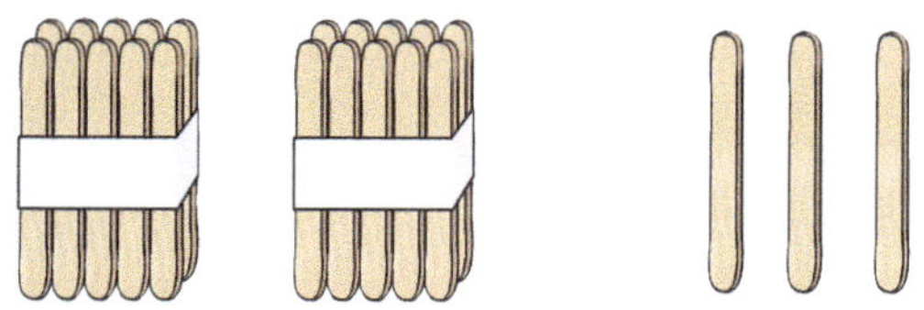

T	O
2	3

32

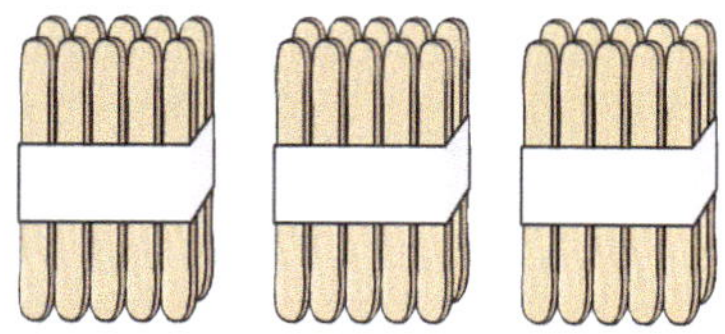

T	O
3	2

The digit **2** → In the number **23**, its **tens place** value is **20**.
In the number **32**, its **ones place** value is **2**.

The digit **3** → In the number **32**, its **tens place** value is **30**
In the number **23**, its **ones place** value is **3**.

Let's Practice

1. Circle the numbers that have a tens place value of 50. Identify

52 25 75 51

85 54 35

2. Look at the red digits. Complete the table. Apply

	Number	Position	Value
	21	ones	1
a.	1		
b.	100		
c.	91		
d.	12		

3. Color the numbers. Interpret

- the digit 8 has a place value of 8
- the digit 5 has a place value of 50
- the digit 7 has a place value of 70

8 53 18 55 5 37 15 85 57 38 87 72 75

4. Count the tens and ones for each number. Answer. Analyze

a.

The number equals ☐ T and ☐ O.

b.

The number equals ☐ T and ☐ O.

c. What numbers are **a** and **b**? a ▶ ☐ b ▶ ☐

d. Does the digit 4 have the same place value in both numbers? Why or why not?

____

____

Did You Know...?

To count tens and ones, you can use blocks.

 ▶ represents 1 **one**

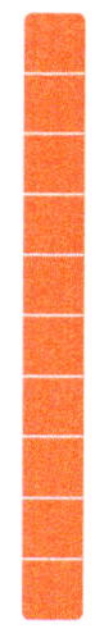 ▶ represents 1 **ten**

5. Read and answer. Analyze

I am thinking of a number with 2 tens and 0 ones.
If I switch the digits, the number becomes 2.

What number am I thinking of? ▶ ☐

Composing and Decomposing Numbers

Let's Connect

John wants to know how many juice boxes he has.

2 tens and 3 ones.

20 + 3 = 23

John has 23 juice boxes.

Let's Learn

Composing a number means solving an addition according to the place value of its digits.

1 **ten** and 6 **ones** 10 + 6

16

Decomposing a number means breaking down a number according to the place value of its digits.

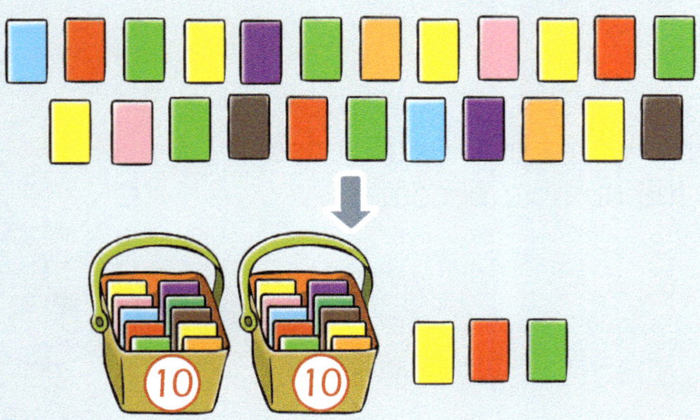

23

2 **tens** and 3 **ones** 20 + 3

Let's Practice

1. Look and complete. Identify

a.

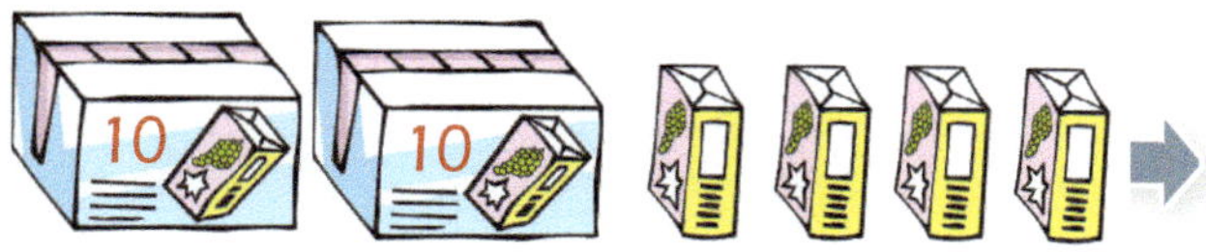

____ tens and ____ ones.

____ + ____ = ____

There are ____ boxes of grape juice.

b.

____ tens and ____ ones.

____ + ____ = ____

There are ____ boxes of pineapple juice.

c.

____ tens and ____ ones.

____ + ____ = ____

There are ____ boxes of strawberry juice.

2. Circle groups of 10 buttons. Complete. Understand

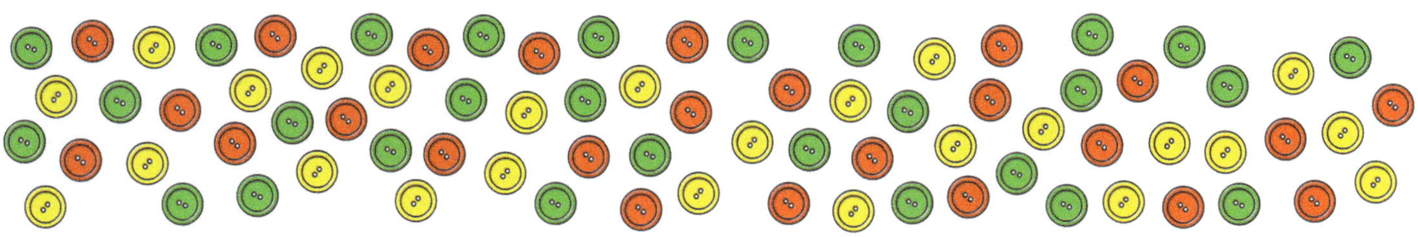

____ tens and ____ ones.

____ + ____ = ____

3. Decompose each number. Apply

a. 47

______ tens and ______ ones.

[ ] + [ ]

b. 76

______ tens and ______ ones.

[ ] + [ ]

c. 98

______ tens and ______ ones.

[ ] + [ ]

4. Read and complete. Analyze

I am a number that has 8 tens and 3 ones. What number am I?

a. ______ tens and ______ ones.

______ + ______ = ______ ➡ The number is [ ].

With a little more I can reach one hundred, but right now I have 9 tens and 9 ones. What number am I?

b.

_____ tens and _____ ones.

_____ + _____ = _____ ➡ The number is ☐.

Quiz Yourself

Answer each word problem.

The number 22 can be represented by 2 groups of 10 objects and 2 more objects.

- Is Julie correct? Mark the correct answer with a ✔.

  Represent the number using ●.

☐ YES

☐ NO

The number 76 has 7 tens and 6 ones.

- Is Matthew correct? Mark the correct answer with a ✔.

  Decompose and explain.

☐ YES

☐ NO

Let's Check!

Ones (1s), Tens (10s) and Hundreds (100s)

1. Circle the fruits with different colors.

2 tens in

8 ones in

4 tens and 5 ones in

Reading and Writing Numbers Up To 100

2. Match each number with its word form.

a.	27	ninety-three
b.	8	twenty-seven
c.	15	fifteen
d.	93	eight

Place Value

3. Read and answer.

a. What is the place value of the digit 6 in the number 46?

The place value is ☐.

b. What is the place value of the digit 6 in the number 64?

The place value is ☐.

Composing and Decomposing Numbers

4. Compose and decompose the numbers.

a. $80 + 1 = \square$

b. $67 = \square + \square$

How Did You Do?

For each color a .

Comparing and Putting Numbers with Different Tens Place Value in Order

Let's Connect

Jenna and Frank want to know who has more ice-cream sticks. They separated the sticks into groups of tens and ones.

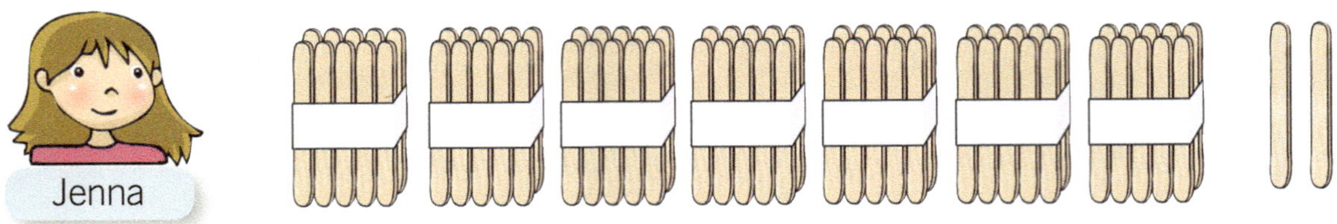

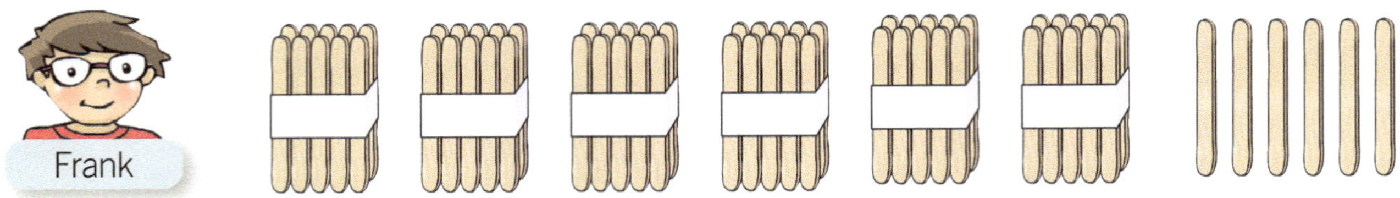

- How many tens do Jenna and Frank have?

 has ☐ tens = ☐ sticks

 has ☐ tens = ☐ sticks

- Who has more tens? ______________________

- How many sticks do Jenna and Frank have?

 has ☐ sticks.  has ☐ sticks.

- Who has more sticks? Complete and circle.

The number ☐ is greater than ☐, so   has more sticks.

Let's Learn

When you **compare** numbers with the same number of digits, compare one digit at a time. Compare digits from left to right. Pay attention to the place value of each digit.

87 → 80 + 7

43 → 40 + 3

80 is **greater than** 40.
40 is **less than** 80.

87 is **greater than** 43.
43 is **less than** 87.

Let's Practice

1. Circle the correct number. Apply

a. the biggest number ➡ 95 88 93

b. the smallest number ➡ 82 71 74

2. Use **Sticker Set 10** on **page 171**. Put the numbers in order from smallest to biggest. Apply

Comparing and Putting Numbers with the Same Tens Place Value in Order

Let's Connect

Jenna wants to know if she has more ice-cream sticks than Justin. To resolve the problem, they separated the sticks into groups of tens and ones.

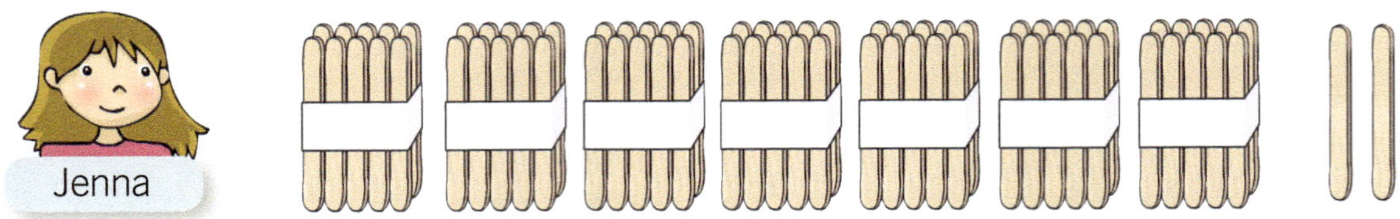

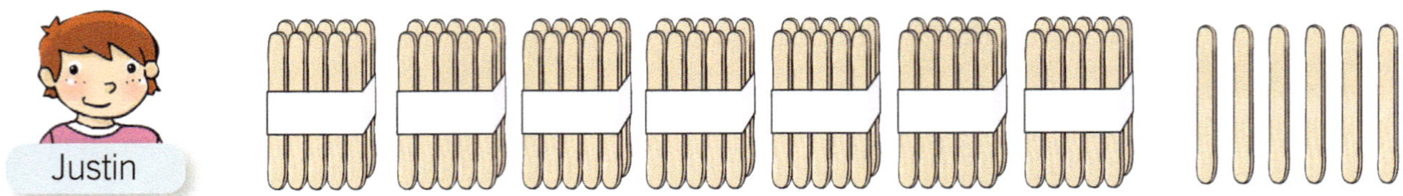

- How many groups of tens do Jenna and Justin have?

 has ☐ tens = ☐ sticks

 has ☐ tens = ☐ sticks

- Who made more groups of ten with the ice-cream sticks? ______________________
- Who has more sticks left? ______________________
- Who has more sticks? Complete and circle.

 has ☐ sticks.  has ☐ sticks.

The number ☐ is greater than ☐, so   has more sticks.

Let's Learn

Sometimes, numbers have the same number of digits and the same tens place value. To **compare** them, look at the ones place.

57 is **greater than** 52.
52 is **less than** 57.

57 → 50 + 7

52 → 50 + 7

50 is **equal** to 50

7 is **greater than** 2
2 is **less than** 7

Let's Practice

1. Color the numbers that have an equal number of tens with the same color. Identify

95 26 67 66 20 99

2. Circle the correct answers. Apply

a. 26 is greater than / less than 20.

b. 66 is greater than / less than 67.

c. 95 is greater than / less than 99.

d. 84 is greater than / less than 82.

Education through Values

You can recycle paper, glass, cardboard and cans, and you can also recycle wood!
Help the environment and save trees!

Estimating Quantities

Let's Connect

Paul wants to know how many strawberries will fit in a . He makes an estimate using a few strawberries as a reference.

referent

Paul knows that there are 5 strawberries in this glass.

- Estimate how many strawberries will fit in the glass.

  I estimate that ☐ strawberries will fit in the glass.

- How did you estimate? Explain.

  ____

  ____

Word Focus

Estimate means to calculate an answer without measuring exactly.

Let's Learn

Use objects you recognize to help you **estimate**. When you know the dimensions of an object you can use it as a **referent**. This helps you estimate quantities better.

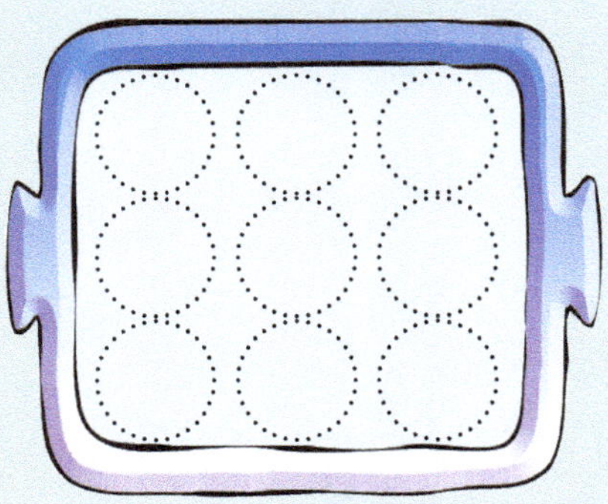

If you look at the size and shape of the orange you can make an estimate. You can estimate that 9 oranges fit on this tray.

Let's Practice

1. Look at the referents. Estimate how many fruits fit on each tray. Apply

a. How many bananas fit on the tray?

____

b. How many apples fit on the tray?

____

Quiz Yourself

Look at the referent and answer.

- How many pears fit on each tray?

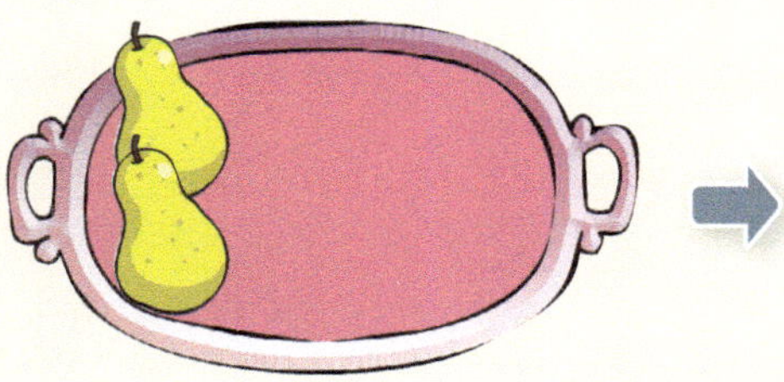

I estimate that __________ pears fit on the tray.

I estimate that __________ pears fit on the tray.

- On which tray do you think more pears fit? Explain.

____

____

Counting From One Addend

Let's Connect

- What type of operation is Maya solving? Circle.

addition subtraction

- How does Maya solve the math operation?

◯ ordering
◯ counting
◯ estimating

The numbers we **add** together are called **addends**. The **sum** is the total.

Let's Learn

Counting from one **addend** is a strategy used to solve addition operations. To solve an operation using this strategy, start counting from one of the addends.

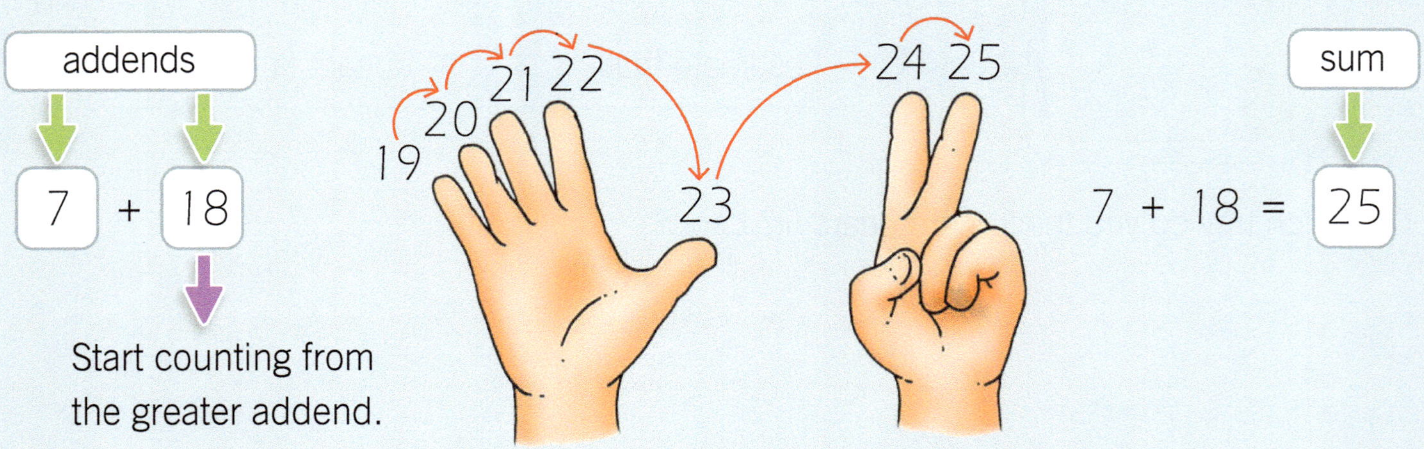

Let's Practice

1. Solve by counting from one addend. Apply

a. 15 + 2 = ☐

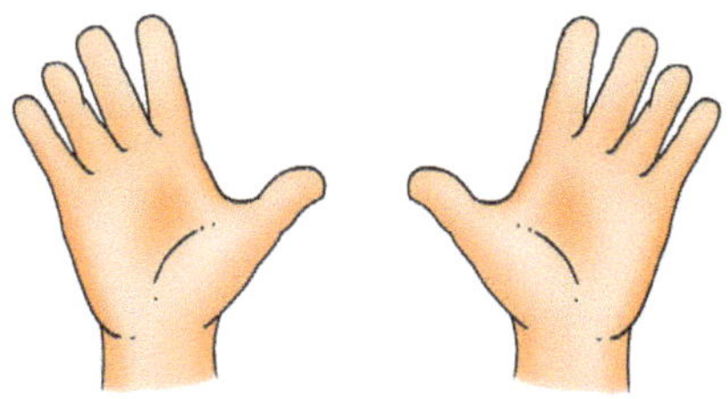

b. 9 + 27 = ☐

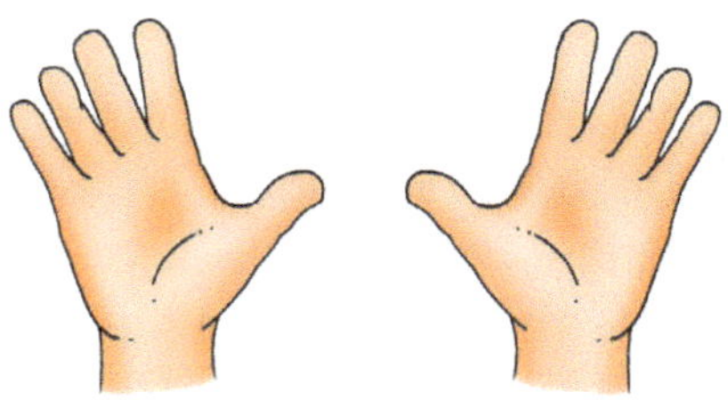

c. 6 + 23 = ☐

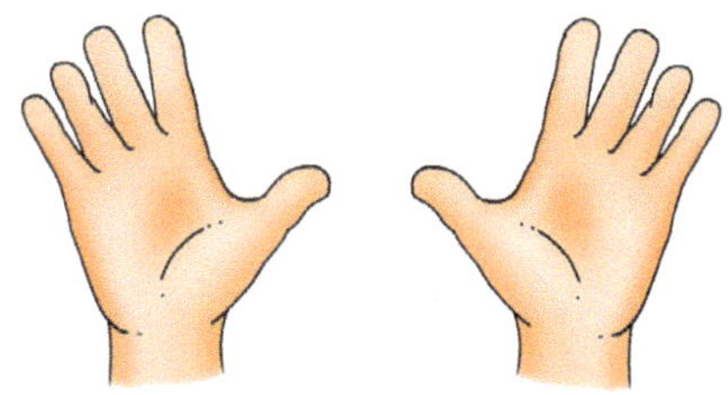

d. 32 + 5 = ☐

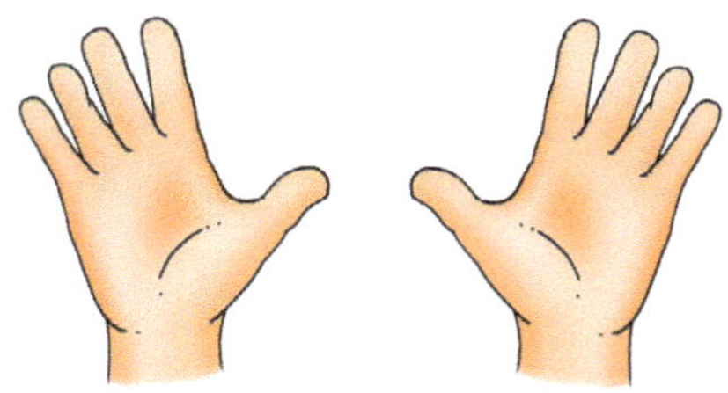

2. Solve by counting from one addend. Apply

a. 

plus 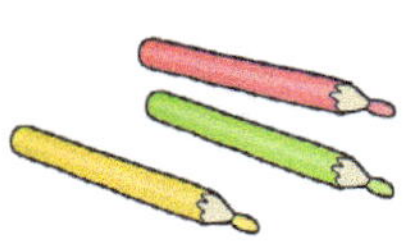 equals ☐ 

b.  plus 

equals ☐ 

c. 

plus  equals ☐ 

Remember!

When counting from one addend to solve addition problems, start with the greater addend.

Counting Backward

Let's Connect

- What type of operation is Dylan solving? Circle.

addition subtraction

- How does Dylan solve the problem?

◯ counting from 1
◯ counting backward
◯ counting forward

The big number that we take away from is called a "minuend" and the number that we take away from it is called a "subtrahend."

Word Focus

The **difference** is the **answer** to a subtraction.

Let's Learn

Counting backward is a strategy you can use to solve subtraction operations. You have to start counting backward from the **minuend**, using as many numbers as the **subtrahend** indicates.

minuend

29 − 8

subtrahend

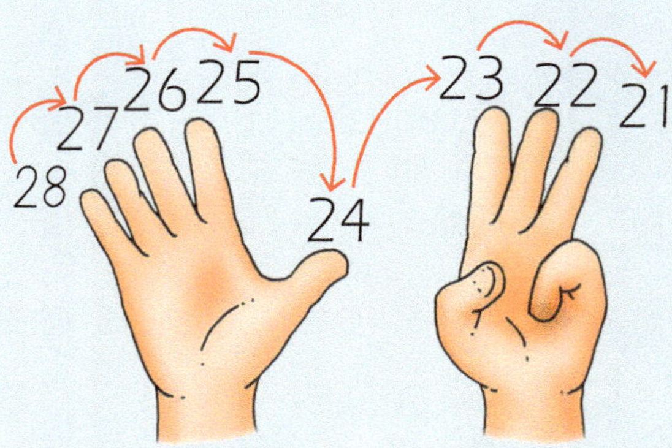

difference

29 − 8 = 21

Let's Practice

1. Solve by counting backward. Apply

a. 48 − 3 = ☐

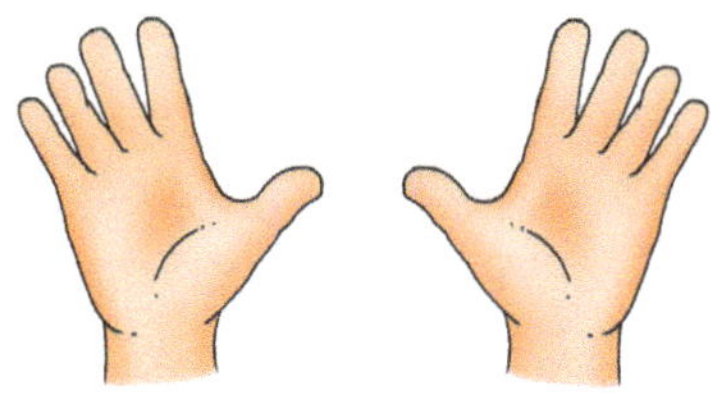

c. 25 − 5 = ☐

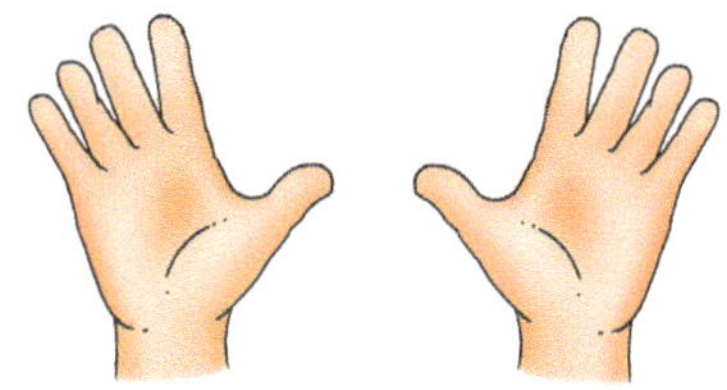

b. 36 − 7 = ☐

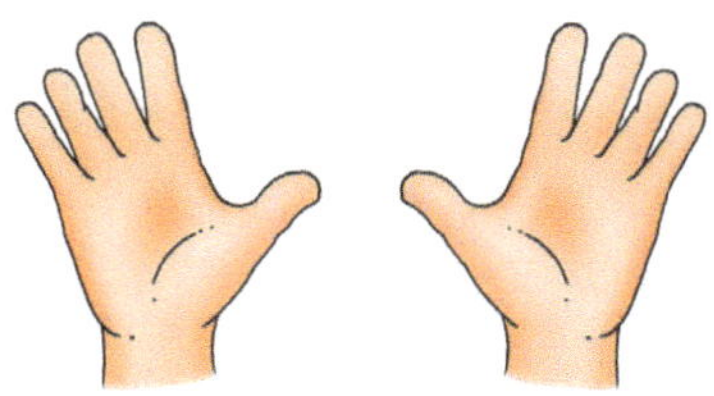

d. 34 − 4 = ☐

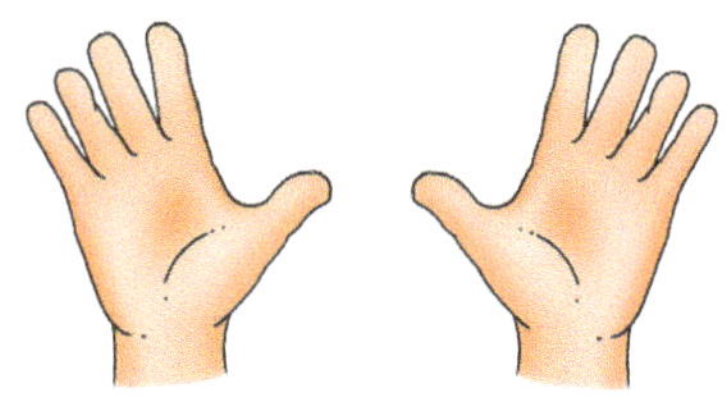

2. Solve by counting backward. Apply

a. 

minus 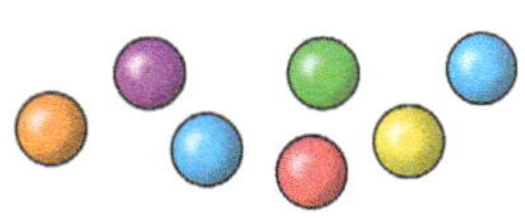 is equal to ☐ 

b. 

minus  is equal to ☐ 

c. 

minus  is equal to ☐ 

Numbered Tape

Let's Connect

- If 41 is the sum and 28 is one addend, what is the other addend? → ☐
- If the circled numbers on the numbered tape are part of a subtraction operation, which one is the minuend? → ☐

Did You Know...?

Numbered tapes, called measuring tapes, are used to measure people for clothing. The tape is flexible so you can accurately measure a person's body.

Let's Learn

You can use a **numbered tape** to solve addition and subtraction operations.

- **addition** $28 + 13 = 41$

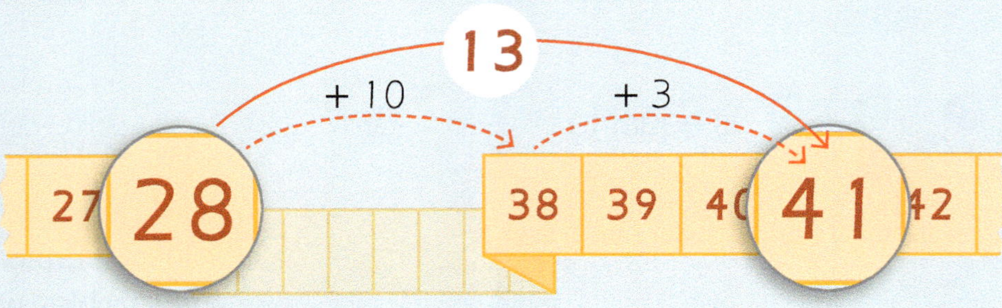

- **subtraction** $41 - 13 = 28$

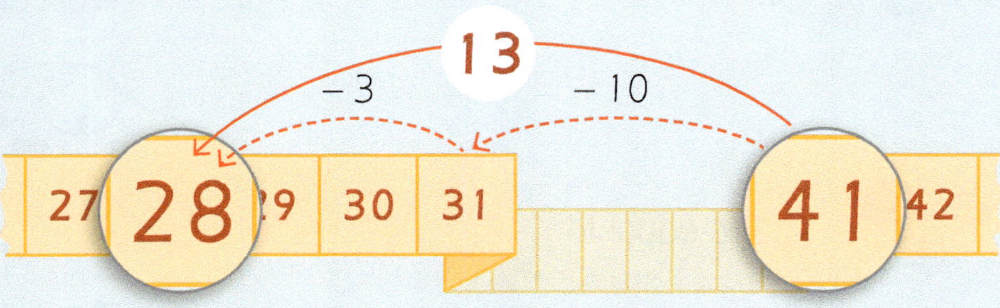

Let's Practice

1. Draw the jumps on the numbered tape and then write the answers. Apply

a. 31 + 17 = ☐

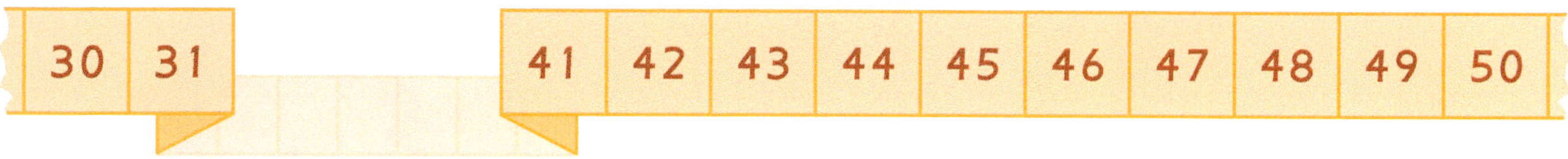

b. 24 + 24 = ☐

c. 23 − 15 = ☐

d. 35 − 25 = ☐

Counting

Let's Connect

- What operation can Bob use to know the total number of marbles he won? Write the operation.

☐ ☐ ☐

- Bob does not have the marbles to count or a paper and pen to write with. How can he solve the operation?

  Write how you would do it.

  ____

  ____

- What operation could you use to check your answer? Write the operation.

☐ ☐ ☐ = ☐

Let's Learn

Adding or subtracting in your head is called a **mental math strategy**.

- **Addition**

  Count **forward**.

  15 + 4

15, 16, 17, 18, **19**

15 + 4 = 19

- **Subtraction**

  Count **backward**.

19, 18, 17, 16, **15**

  19 − 4

19 − 4 = 15

Let's Practice

1. Match the operations with the answers. Relate

35 − 5	45
11 + 4	15
19 − 3	30
40 + 5	16
26 − 2	24

Tip

Counting in your head is easier if you use your fingers or imagine objects.

Exam Strategies

Look and Learn

Mark the correct answer with an ✗.

1 Emily says to Lucy, “I am thinking of a number that is greater than 66 and less than 68.”

What number is Emily thinking of?

- A 65
- B 67 ☒
- C 69

Read the word problem carefully.

Read the question and think about the answer.

Look for the answer. Mark it with an ✗.

Your Turn!

Mark the correct answer with an ✗.

2 Lucy says to Emily, “I am thinking of a number that is less than 75 and greater than 73.”

What number is Lucy thinking of?

- A 74
- B 76
- C 77

What Did You Learn?

Final Evaluation

Reading and Writing Numbers Up To 100

1. Match each number with its word form.

a. 25

b. 64

c. 18

d. 37

thirty-seven

twenty-five

sixty-four

eighteen

Comparing and Putting Numbers in Order

2. Look at the picture and answer.

a. Write a number greater than George's number. ▶ ☐

b. Write a number less than Natalie's number and greater than 90. ▶ ☐

c. Who has the biggest number? Who has the smallest number?

____

Composing and Decomposing Numbers

3. Decompose the number 63 and mark the correct answer with an **X**.

63
6 **T** + 3 **O**
6 + 3

63
6 **T** + 3 **O**
60 + 3

Estimating Quantities

4. Read carefully. Use the picture to solve the word problem.

Zoe needs to deposit a check in the bank. There is a long line of people.

a. Count how many people are in the circled section.

There are ☐ people.

b. Estimate how many people are in front of Zoe in the line?

I estimate that ☐ people are in front of Zoe.

Mark the answers with an ✕.

Use the picture to answer questions 5 and 6.

5. Order from greatest to smallest according to the number of cans.

A Jessica, Geoff, Hannah

B Hannah, Jessica, Geoff

C Geoff, Jessica, Hannah

---

6. Who has a 6 in the ones place?

A Hannah

B Jessica

C Geoff

Find Test 2 Study Page

How Did You Do?

For each 🐸 color a ⬭.

Unit 3

Measurement, Geometry and Data

Key Words

on / under

two-dimensional shapes

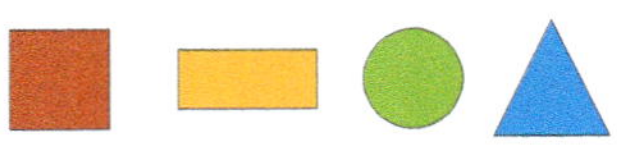

side

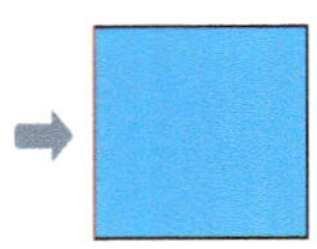

vertex

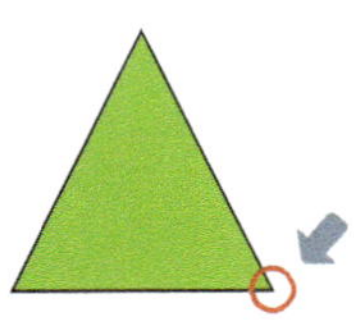

In this unit you will learn to:

- identify the position of objects and people in relation to other objects and people.
- identify days, months and dates on a calendar.
- measure using your body and other objects.
- describe, compare and draw geometric shapes.
- collect, record and interpret data using tables and block charts.
- use creative math skills for problem solving.

What Do You Know? Initial Evaluation

Look at the picture and answer.

1. Draw two more toys on the floor.

2. Look at the picture. Is the "Height Measurements" wall on the left or right?

____

3. What would you use to find out who is the tallest child?

____

4. Circle the two-dimensional shapes in the picture. Write their names.

a. ○ _______________

b. △ _______________

c. □ _______________

d. ▭ _______________

5. How many children are in the classroom? Complete the table.

Children in the Classroom		
	Girls	Boys
Number		

Position of Objects and People

Let's Connect

Neil and Paula are looking for objects on the shelves in the classroom.

- Is Neil correct?

  Yes No , because ______________________________.

- What other points of reference could Neil give Paula?

  ____

- What is behind the shelves?

  ____

- What is on the shelves to the left?

  ____

- How many balls of yarn are outside the box? ▶ ☐ balls of yarn.

Let's Learn

To describe the position of objects or people around us, we can use:

on the left / right

on / under

in front of / behind

inside / outside

Challenge

Play "Simon Says." Use the position words and play with your friends!

Let's Practice

1. Use **Cutout 1** on **page 155**. Glue the images in the correct places on the picture. Apply

1. Laura is sitting on the left of Martin.
2. There is a book on the table.
3.  is under the table.
4. The blocks are inside the box.

Days, Months and Dates on a Calendar

Let's Connect

2019

JANUARY

M	T	W	T	F	S	S
	1	2	3	4	5	6
7	8	9	10	11	12	13
14	15	16	17	18	19	20
21	22	23	24	25	26	27
28	29	30	31			

FEBRUARY

M	T	W	T	F	S	S
				1	2	3
4	5	6	7	8	9	10
11	12	13	14	15	16	17
18	19	20	21	22	23	24
25	26	27	28			

MARCH

M	T	W	T	F	S	S
				1	2	3
4	5	6	7	8	9	10
11	12	13	14	15	16	17
18	19	20	21	22	23	24
25	26	27	28	29	30	31

APRIL

M	T	W	T	F	S	S
1	2	3	4	5	6	7
8	9	10	11	12	13	14
15	16	17	18	19	20	21
22	23	24	25	26	27	28
29	30					

MAY

M	T	W	T	F	S	S
		1	2	3	4	5
6	7	8	9	10	11	12
13	14	15	16	17	18	19
20	21	22	23	24	25	26
27	28	29	30	31		

JUNE

M	T	W	T	F	S	S
					1	2
3	4	5	6	7	8	9
10	11	12	13	14	15	16
17	18	19	20	21	22	23
24	25	26	27	28	29	30

JULY

M	T	W	T	F	S	S
1	2	3	**4**	5	6	7
8	9	10	11	12	13	14
15	16	17	18	19	20	21
22	23	24	25	26	27	28
29	30	31				

AUGUST

M	T	W	T	F	S	S
			1	2	3	4
5	6	7	8	9	10	11
12	13	14	15	16	17	18
19	20	21	22	23	24	25
26	27	28	29	30	31	

SEPTEMBER

M	T	W	Th	F	Sa	S
						1
2	3	4	5	6	7	8
9	10	11	12	13	14	15
16	17	18	19	20	21	22
23	24	25	26	27	28	29
30						

OCTOBER

M	T	W	T	F	S	S
	1	2	3	4	5	6
7	8	9	10	11	12	13
14	15	16	17	18	19	20
21	22	23	24	25	26	27
28	29	30	31			

NOVEMBER

M	T	W	T	F	S	S
				1	2	3
4	5	6	7	8	9	10
11	12	13	14	15	16	17
18	19	20	21	22	23	24
25	26	27	**28**	29	30	

DECEMBER

M	T	W	T	F	S	S
						1
2	3	4	5	6	7	8
9	10	11	12	13	14	15
16	17	18	19	20	21	22
23	24	**25**	26	27	28	29
30	31					

- What year does the calendar show?

1998 2003 2019 2023

- What month is your birthday in?

____

- Mark your birthday with your favorite color. On what day of the week is your birthday on the calendar?

____

- Is your birthday on the same day of the week every year? Discuss.

Fun Fact!

In the USA, the week begins on Sunday and in Mexico it begins on Monday.

Some calendars highlight holidays and festivities.

Let's Learn

A calendar shows the 12 months of the year in an organized way. Using a calendar you can identify **dates** as days, months and years.

Follow the steps to find March 3rd on the calendar.

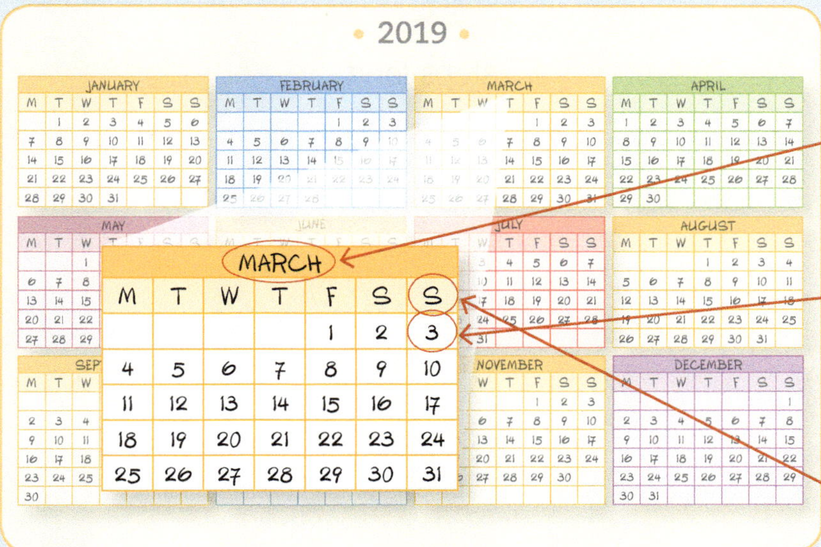

First, locate the **month** – March.

Second, look for the **day** – the 3rd.

Third, locate the **day of the week** – Sunday.

A calendar or planner can help you organize your daily activities and plan your homework.

Let's Practice

1. Use the calendar on **page 74** to answer the questions. Identify

a. What day of the week is August 21st?

___

b. Is there a holiday in December? What holidays does your country celebrate?

___

c. In January, Alice went to a swimming class every Thursday. How many days did she go to class?

Alice went to ☐ swimming classes in January.

Tip

Days of the week are capitalized in English.

Measuring With Your Body and Objects

Let's Connect

Mark and Antonia are measuring the length of the classroom.

- Why are Mark and Antonia's measurements different? Explain.

___

- What other way could you measure the room? Explain.

___

Word Focus

To **standardize** is to measure things the same way.

Let's Learn

You can use objects or parts of your body as **units of measurement**. However, these units of measurements are **not standardized** or consistent. Examples of these units of measurement are an eraser, a sharpener, your hand or your foot.

Let's Practice

1. Measure objects in your classroom using an ice-cream stick as a unit of measurement. Apply

ice-cream stick 

a. A table

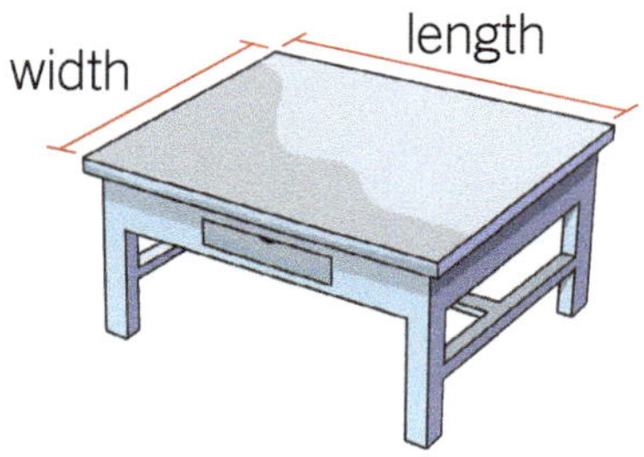

width ▶ ☐ ice-cream sticks

length ▶ ☐ ice-cream sticks

b. A math textbook

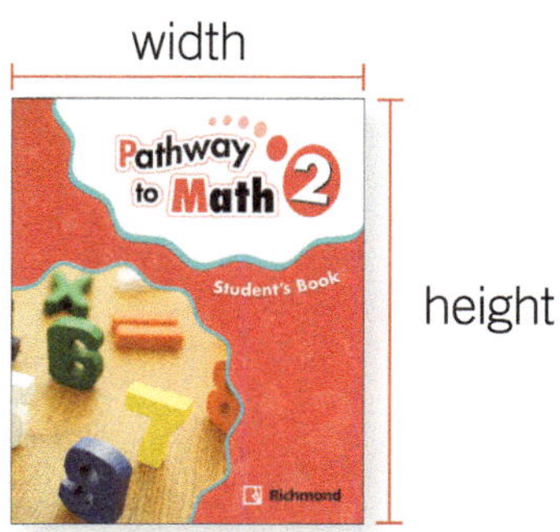

width ▶ ☐ ice-cream sticks

height ▶ ☐ ice-cream sticks

2. Measure the objects in your classroom using the unit of measurement indicated. Apply

a. The classroom door, using your .

width ▶ ☐ 

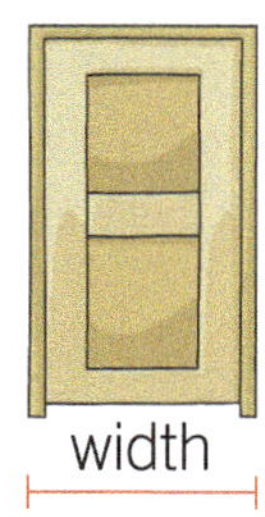

---

b. The whiteboard, using your 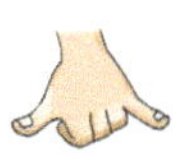.

height ▶ ☐  width ▶ ☐ 

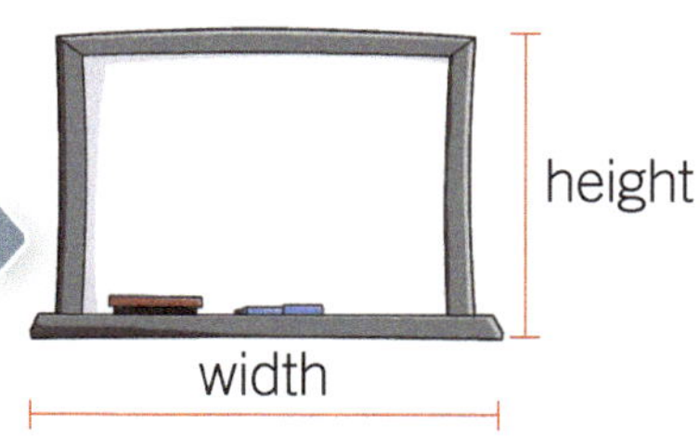

---

c. A pencil case, using a 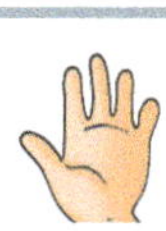.

width ▶ ☐ 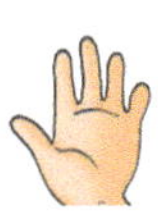 length ▶ ☐ 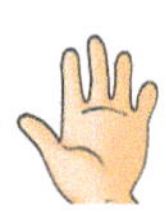

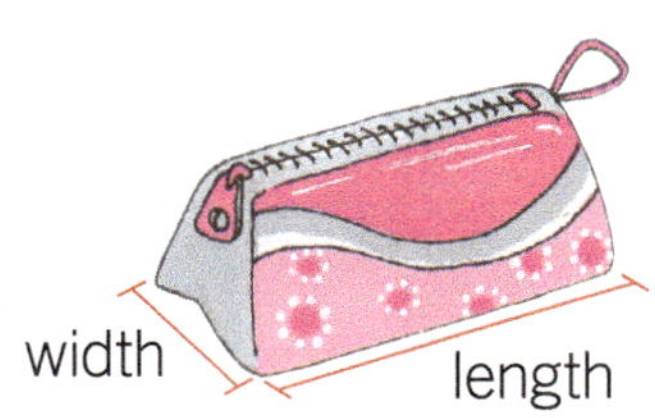

Two-Dimensional Shapes

Let's Connect

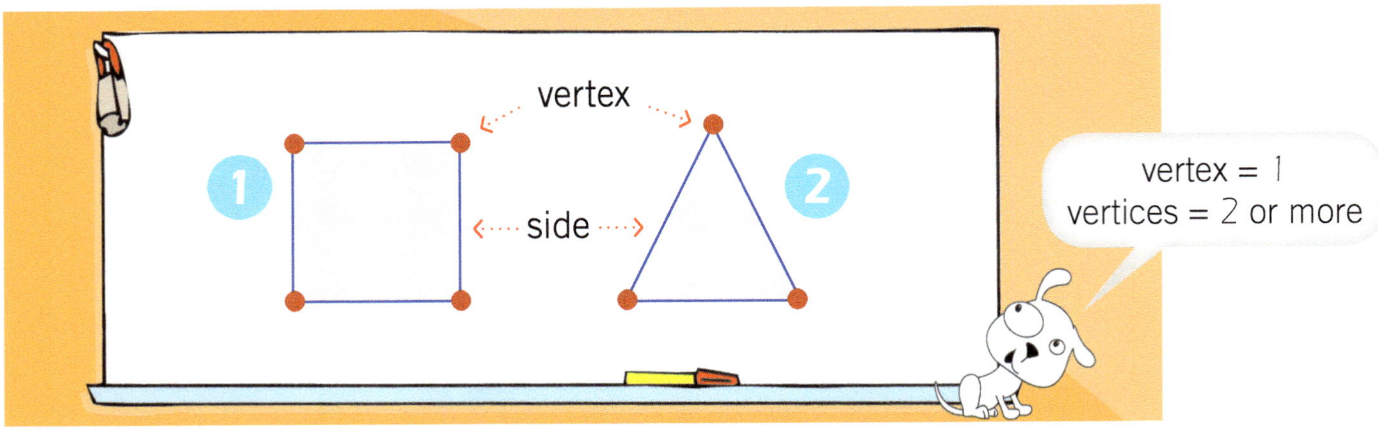

- What are the names of the shapes on the board?

____

- What characteristic of shapes is highlighted in red?

____

- What characteristic of shapes is highlighted in blue?

____

- Look at the picture and complete the sentences.

Shape 1 is a ______________. It has ☐ vertices and ☐ sides.

Shape 2 is a ______________. It has ☐ vertices and ☐ sides.

- What is the difference between the descriptions of the shapes 1 and 2? Explain.

____

____

Let's Learn

Two-dimensional or **geometric shapes** can be described using their characteristics. We can describe their **sides** and **vertices**.

square

It has 4 equal **sides**.
It has 4 **vertices**.

rectangle

It has 2 pairs of equal **sides**.
It has 4 **vertices**.

circle

It has no **sides**.
It has no **vertices**.

triangle

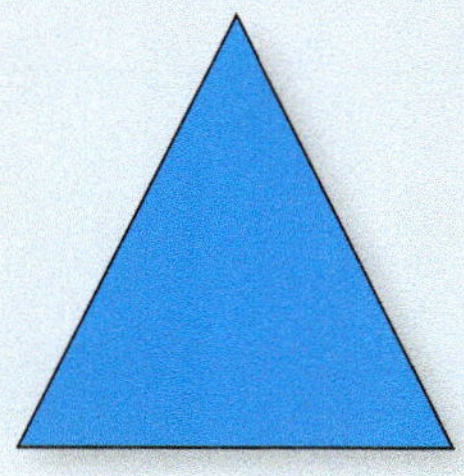

It has 3 **sides**.
It has 3 **vertices**.

Let's Practice

1. Mark the vertices of the shapes in the Let's Learn section in . Trace the sides in .

2. Write the names of the two-dimensional shapes and are thinking of. Analyze

a.

This shape has 4 sides that are all the same.

answer ▶ ______________________

b.

This shape has no sides.

answer ▶ ______________________

Comparing Two-Dimensional Shapes

Let's Connect

The teacher asked students to compare a rectangle and a triangle. Daniel and Sophie are talking about the similarities and differences.

- What other similarities can you identify between a rectangle and a triangle?

____

- What other differences can you identify between a rectangle and a triangle?

____

Let's Learn

To compare **two-dimensional shapes**, we need to look at their properties.

Sides	Vertices
• number of sides • if they are of equal length	• number of vertices

Let's Practice

1. Compare the two-dimensional shapes. Mark the correct sentences with a ✔. Mark the incorrect sentences with an ✘. Compare

a.

- [ ] Both shapes have sides.
- [ ] The rectangle has 3 sides and the triangle has 4 sides.
- [ ] Both shapes have an equal number of vertices.

b.

- [ ] Both shapes have sides.
- [ ] The square has 4 sides.
- [ ] Both shapes have an equal number of vertices.

2. Answer the word problem. Analyze

What do a triangle, a square and a rectangle have in common? Explain.

____

____

Making Two-Dimensional Shapes

Let's Connect

Martha is folding and cutting pieces of paper to make two-dimensional shapes.

- What shape was Martha's piece of paper before she folded it?

____

- How many shapes are there after she folds the paper? ____________

- What shapes does she make after cutting the paper?

____

Let's Learn

You can make different two-dimensional shapes by putting two or more geometric shapes together.

For example: You can make a square with two triangles.

Let's Practice

1. Use **Cutout 2** on **page 155** to complete the activities. Apply

a.

Step 1: Select the square.

Step 2: Fold it into 4 smaller squares.

Step 3: Cut out the squares.

Step 4: Glue the 4 squares in the box.

b.

Step 1: Select the triangle.

Step 2: Fold it into 3 smaller triangles.

Step 3: Cut out the triangles.

Step 4: Glue the 3 triangles in the box.

Quiz Yourself

Draw the two-dimensional shape that fits the description.

- It has more sides than a triangle.
- It can make two triangles.
- It has four equal sides.

Let's Check!

Position of Objects and People

1. Look at the picture and answer.

a. What objects are behind the teacher?

____

b. What objects are on the teacher's table?

____

c. What do you see under the table?

____

Measuring With Your Body and Objects

2. Measure your school bag using a finger as a unit of measurement.

width ▶ [ ] fingers

height ▶ [ ] fingers

3. Write the names of two things you can measure using each body part or object.

a.

Foot ▶ ______________________________

Hand ▶ ______________________________

b.

Eraser ▶ ______________________________

Pencil ▶ ______________________________

4. Which geometric shape has 4 equal sides and 4 equal vertices?

A A square

B A rectangle

C A circle

5. Which sentence is correct?

A Circles and triangles have sides.

B Circles have 1 vertex and triangles have 3.

C Circles do not have any sides and triangles have 3 sides.

How Did You Do?

For each ☺ color a ⬭.

Collecting Data

Let's Connect

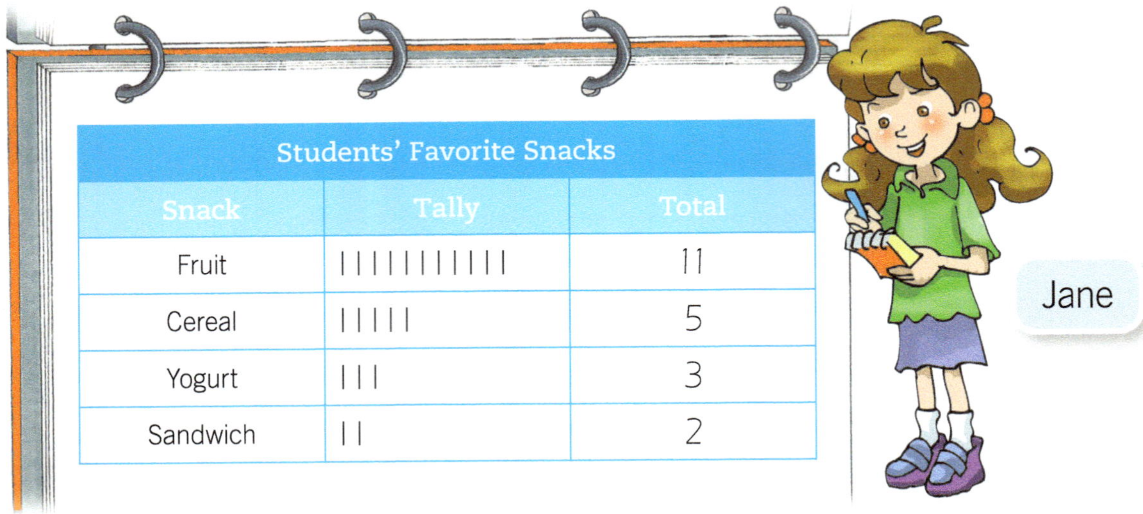

<table>
<tr><th colspan="3">Students' Favorite Snacks</th></tr>
<tr><th>Snack</th><th>Tally</th><th>Total</th></tr>
<tr><td>Fruit</td><td>| | | | | | | | | | |</td><td>11</td></tr>
<tr><td>Cereal</td><td>| | | | |</td><td>5</td></tr>
<tr><td>Yogurt</td><td>| | |</td><td>3</td></tr>
<tr><td>Sandwich</td><td>| |</td><td>2</td></tr>
</table>

- What question do you think Jane asked?

____

- Where did Jane write the answers? Why?

____

- What does | mean in the "Tally" column?

____

- Write the number of students who prefer each snack.

fruit	cereal	yogurt	sandwich
↓	↓	↓	↓
☐	☐	☐	☐

Remember!

The title of a table tells you what question was asked.

Word Focus

A **survey** collects information about an issue or topic. It usually involves questions.

Let's Learn

Tables help you collect and **record** data.

For example, when a group of students were surveyed about their favorite sport, the data was recorded in a table.

Favorite Sport		
Sport	Tally	Total
Soccer	I I I I I I I I I I I	11
Swimming	I I I I I I I I I I I I I I	14

You can record data with tally marks like ✗, ✔ or **I**. Then you can count the marks to find the total.

Let's Practice

1. Look at the picture. Record the data you see in the table. Apply

Vacation Destination		
Destination	Tally	Total

Interpreting Data in a Table

Let's Connect

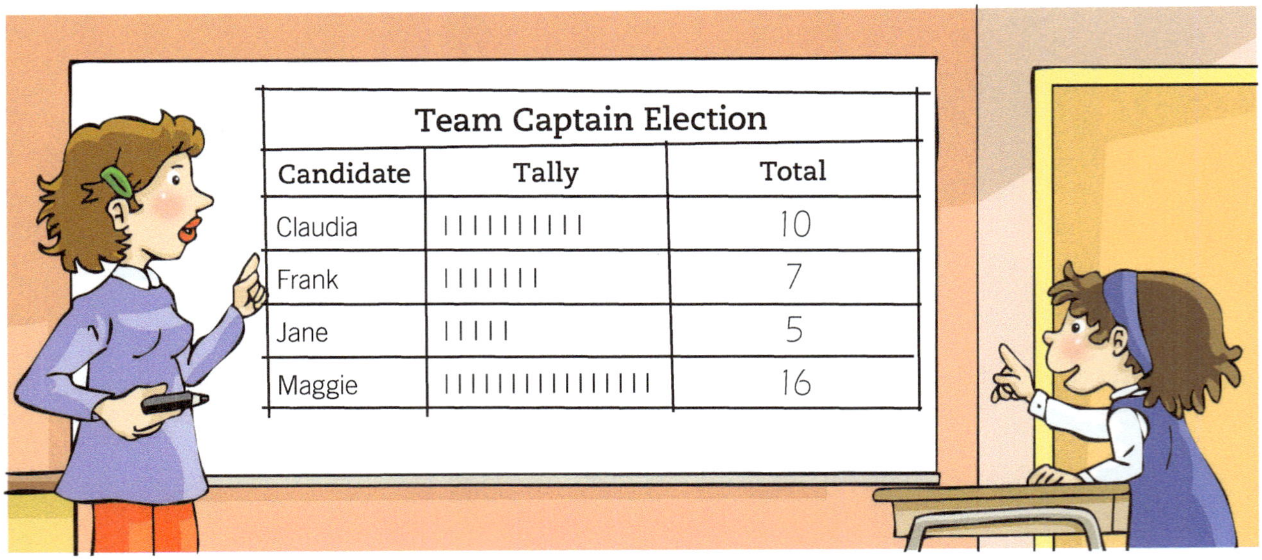

<table>
<tr><th colspan="3">Team Captain Election</th></tr>
<tr><th>Candidate</th><th>Tally</th><th>Total</th></tr>
<tr><td>Claudia</td><td>||||||||||</td><td>10</td></tr>
<tr><td>Frank</td><td>|||||||</td><td>7</td></tr>
<tr><td>Jane</td><td>|||||</td><td>5</td></tr>
<tr><td>Maggie</td><td>||||||||||||||||</td><td>16</td></tr>
</table>

Word Focus

An **election** is a process where people choose a representative by voting.

- Which student got the least votes?

  ____________________, because she got [ ] votes.

- Put the candidates in order by the number of votes they got, from most to least.

  ________________, ________________, ________________ and ________________.

- Who was elected team captain?

  ____

- Can you tell how many students voted? Explain.

  ____

  ____

Education through Values

Voting to choose a leader is a democratic way to make a decision.

Let's Learn

Tables present information in an organized way and help us **interpret** data.

Class President Election		
Candidate	Tally	Total
Lauren	|||||||||||||	13
Michael	||||||	6
Meryl	||||||||||||||||	16

The class president will be Meryl, because she got the most votes.

Let's Practice

1. Answer using the data in the table. Interpret

Students from second grade registered for sports teams.

Number of Students Registered		
Category	Tally	Total
Beginner	||||||||||||	12
Intermediate	|||||||||||||||	15
Advanced	||||||||||	10

- In which category did most students register?

____

- How many students registered in total? ▶ ☐ students

2. Answer using the data in the table. Interpret

Some students from 2nd grade were surveyed about their favorite subjects.

Favorite Subject		
Subject	**Tally**	**Total**
Computer Science	I I I I	4
Math	I I I I I I I I I	9
Physical Education	I I I I I I I	7
Science	I I I I I I	6

a. What is the title of the table?

____

b. What question do you think the survey asked? Write it.

____?

Fun Fact!

The word **tally** comes from the Latin word for very small stick or twig. People used to count with twigs in the past.

c. How many 2nd grade students answered the question?

d. Which is the most popular subject?

____

e. Can you tell how many students preferred English? Explain.

Yes No, because ____

____.

Recording Data in Block Charts

Let's Connect

- How many cars of each color are there?

▶ ☐ ▶ ☐ ▶ ☐

- Color a block for each car of each color.

Number of Cars by Color

Red	Green	Blue

Let's Learn

Block charts help you record data. The blocks are colored according to the number of elements in each category.

For example, of the twenty students in 2nd grade, eight are 7 years old and twelve are 8 years old.

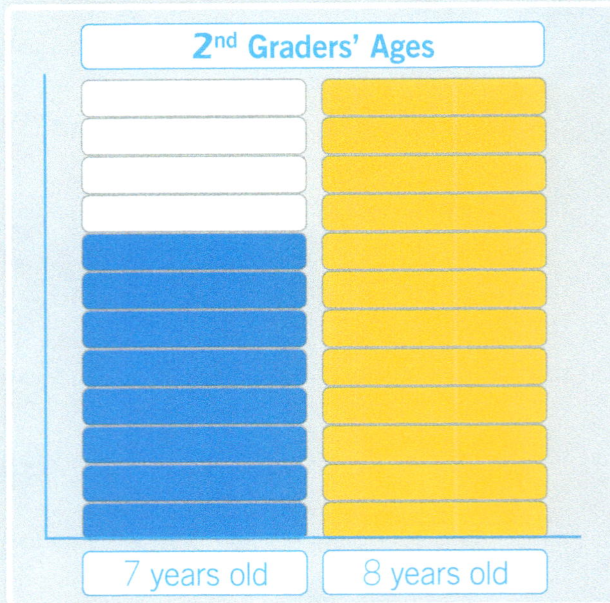

Let's Practice

1. Represent the data in a block chart. Apply

Some 2nd graders were asked to name their favorite pet.
9 said dogs, 4 said cats and 6 said fish.

2. Follow the steps to complete the activity. Apply

Step 1: Ask 15 classmates the question:

"In which month is your birthday?"

Step 2: Record the answers in the table.

Birthdays of 15 Classmates					
Month	**Tally**	**Total**	**Month**	**Tally**	**Total**
January			July		
February			August		
March			September		
April			October		
May			November		
June			December		

Step 3: Complete the block chart with the data you collected.

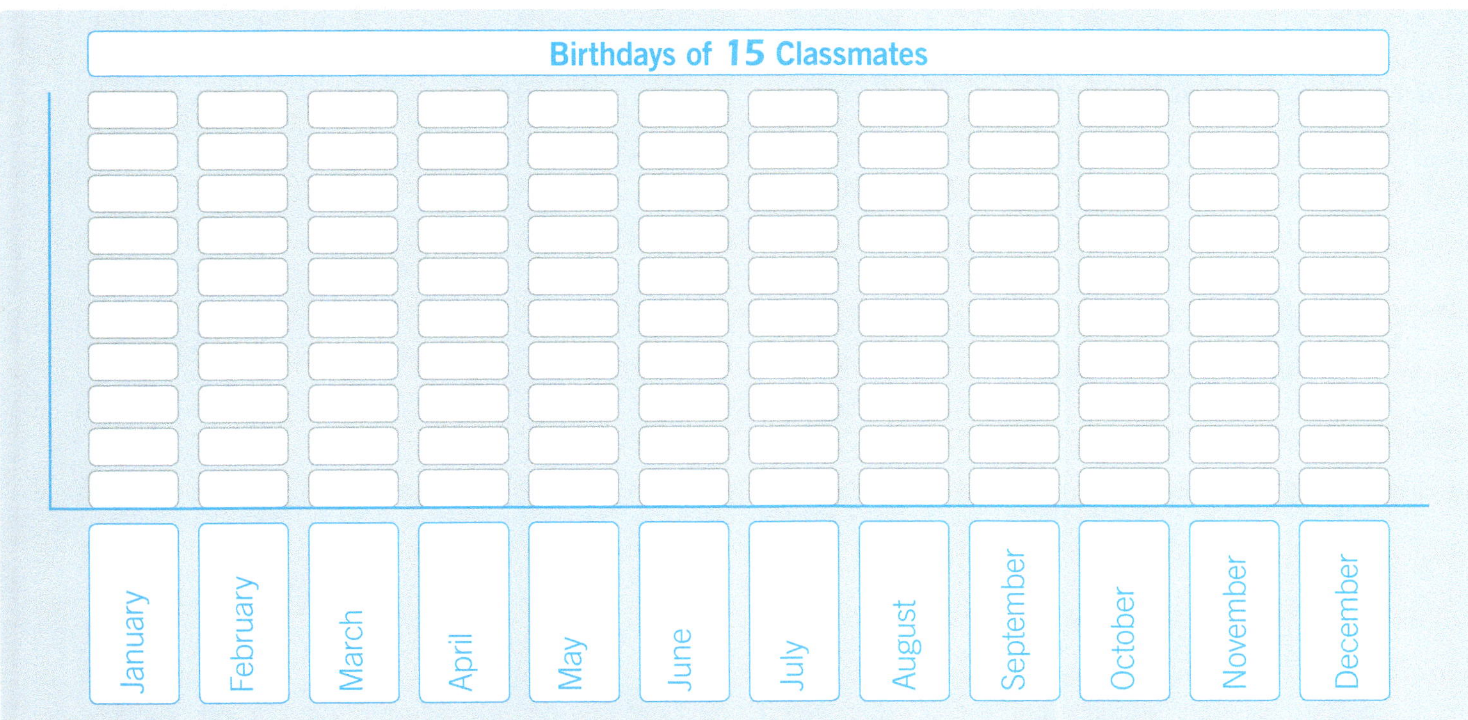

Exam Strategies

Look and Learn

Mark the correct answer with an X .

1 Which shape is a triangle?

Read the word problem carefully.

[A] 

[B] 

Look at the options and determine which answer is correct.

[C] (marked with an X) 

Mark your answer with an X .

Your Turn!

Mark the correct answer with an X .

2 Which shape does not have equal sides?

[A] 

[B] 

[C] 

What Did You Learn?

Final Evaluation

Days, Months and Dates on a Calendar

1. Circle the month that has 31 days.

FEBRUARY

M	T	W	T	F	S	S
				1	2	3
4	5	6	7	8	9	10
11	12	13	14	15	16	17
18	19	20	21	22	23	24
25	26	27	28			

JUNE

M	T	W	T	F	S	S
					1	2
3	4	5	6	7	8	9
10	11	12	13	14	15	16
17	18	19	20	21	22	23
24	25	26	27	28	29	30

JULY

M	T	W	T	F	S	S
1	2	3	4	5	6	7
8	9	10	11	12	13	14
15	16	17	18	19	20	21
22	23	24	25	26	27	28
29	30	31				

NOVEMBER

M	T	W	T	F	S	S
				1	2	3
4	5	6	7	8	9	10
11	12	13	14	15	16	17
18	19	20	21	22	23	24
25	26	27	28	29	30	

Measure Using Your Body and Objects

2. Measure the height and width using a paper clip.

a.

clips

b.

clips

Recording Data in a Block Chart

3. Look at the tokens. Complete the block chart with information.

Two-Dimensional Shapes

4. Compare the shapes. Write one similarity and one difference between them.

	Shape	Similarity	Difference
a.			
b.	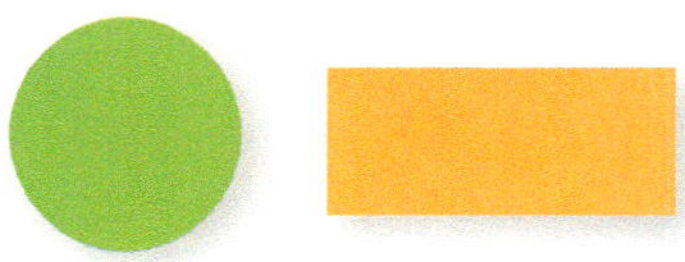		
c.			

Mark the correct answer with an ✕ .

Use the calendar to answer <u>questions 5 – 7</u>.

2016

August						
M	T	W	T	F	S	S
1	2	3	4	5	6	7
8	9	10	11	12	13	14
15	16	17	18	19	20	21
22	23	24	25	26	27	28
29	30	31				

5. What day of the week does August 2016 start on?

A Monday

B Thursday

C Friday

6. How many Thursdays are there in August 2016?

A 4

B 5

C 9

7. What day of the week is August 7th?

A Tuesday

B Saturday

C Sunday

Find Test 3 Study Page

How Did You Do?

For each (smiling frog) color a (lily pad).

Unit 4

Numbers and Operations Up To 1,000

Key Words

digit

1, 2, 3, ...

compose / decompose

300 + 40 + 9 → 349

349 → 300 + 40 + 9

adding in columns

	H	T	O
	4	2	1
+	2	3	5
	6	5	6

In this unit you will learn to:

- count, read and write numbers up to 1,000.
- understand place value with hundreds.
- compose and decompose numbers up to 1,000.
- use math strategies to solve addition and subtraction problems.
- work in a clear and organized way.

What Do You Know? Initial Evaluation

Look at the picture and answer.

1. What is the price of one kilogram of bananas?

   ____ ¢

2. How many children are there?

   There are ____ children.

3. How many adults are there?

   There are ____ adults.

4. How many people are at the market in total?

5. How many more adults than children are at the market?

6. Mark the correct sentence with a ✓.

   ____ The number of children is greater than the number of adults.

   ____ The number of children is smaller than the number of adults.

7. Circle any numbers you do not know in the picture. Discuss them with a partner.

Section
1 Numbers Up To 1,000

Reading and Writing Numbers Up To 1,000

Let's Connect

- What information do you need to know if Alice has the winning raffle ticket?

____

Tip

Sentence starter:
I need to know...

- How many hundreds, tens and ones does Alice's raffle ticket have?

H	T	O

- What digit is in the hundreds place?

The digit ☐ is in the hundreds place.

- Who has the winning raffle ticket? How do you know? Explain.

____

____

Let's Learn

To read numbers with 3 digits, you start with the digit, in the **hundreds**, then the digit in the **tens** and finally, the digit in the **ones** place.

The digit in the hundreds place can have these values:

1 ▶ one hundred	4 ▶ four hundred	7 ▶ seven hundred
2 ▶ two hundred	5 ▶ five hundred	8 ▶ eight hundred
3 ▶ three hundred	6 ▶ six hundred	9 ▶ nine hundred

Hundreds	Tens	Ones
3	6	8

So, 368 is three hundred sixty-eight.

Let's Practice

1. Write the word forms of the red digits. Understand

a. 258 ▶ The digit in the hundreds place is written ______________________.

b. 854 ▶ The digit in the hundreds place is written ______________________.

2. Write the word forms of the numbers. Represent

a. 354 ▶ ____.

b. 953 ▶ ____.

c. 541 ▶ ____.

Counting by 100s Up To 1,000

Let's Connect

Challenge

Combine blocks with a partner. How many ways can you arrange them? What flat shapes can you make?

- How many squares does each child have?

  Each child has ☐ squares.

- How did Dan count? What numbers did he say out loud?

  He counted by ☐ and said the numbers ☐, ☐ and ☐.

- Mark the place value that changes with a ✓.

  ☐ hundreds ☐ tens ☐ units

- If Milton had 124 squares and Karen and Dan had 100 each. How would Dan count the squares?

Let's Learn

When **counting by 100s**, the digit in the hundreds place changes.

Counting **forward** by 100s.

118, 218, 318, 418, 518

Counting **backward** by 100s.

625, 525, 425, 325, 225

Let's Practice

1. Complete by counting forward or backward. Understand

a. 0, 100, 200, 300, 400, ____

b. 853, 753, 653, 553, 453, ____

c. 95, 195, 295, 395, 495, ____

2. Count by 100s to complete. Apply

a. Start with 965 and count backward.

965, ____, ____, ____, ____, ____

b. Start with 354 and count forward.

354, ____, ____, ____, ____, ____

Hundreds and Thousands

Let's Connect

- How many ones are there in the teacher's number square? ▶ ☐ ones
- How many tens are in the teacher's number square? ▶ ☐ tens
- How many number squares are on the table? ▶ ☐ number squares
- How many ones are on the table? ▶ ☐ ones
- The children say that ten number squares equal 1,000? Are they correct? Explain.

____

____

Let's Learn

1 thousand

1 hundred

one thousand equals
- ten hundreds
- one hundred tens
- one thousand ones

Let's Practice

Did You Know...?

The **thousands place value** is represented by **Th**.

1. Use the number squares in **Cutout 3** on **page 157** to represent the answer. Represent

4 hundreds and 2 tens

Place Value

Let's Connect

George is representing a number using squares.

- How many hundreds or groups of 100 did George make?

  He made ☐ hundreds, which equals 500 ones.

- How many tens did George make?

  He made ☐ tens, which equals 40 ones.

- How many ones are left?

  ☐ ones are left.

- What number did George represent with the squares?

  He represented the number ☐.

- George thinks he can use the same number of ☐ (ones) to represent the number 745. Do you agree?

  (Yes) (No), because ______________________________

  ______________________________.

Let's Learn

321 and 132 have the same digits, but they are represented differently:

H	T	O
3	2	1

H	T	O
1	3	2

The digit 3
- ➡ is in the **hundreds place** with a place value of **300** in the number **321**.
- ➡ is in the **tens place** with a place value of **30** in the number **132**.

The digit 1
- ➡ is in the **ones place** with a place value of **1** in the number **321**.
- ➡ is in the **hundreds place** with a place value of **100** in the number **132**.

Let's Practice

1. Complete the table according to the red digits. Apply

	Number	Position	Value
a.	258		
b.	655		
c.	931		
d.	1,000		

Composing and Decomposing Numbers

Let's Connect

Teresa and Carl are making numbers with number cards.

- What number cards did Teresa use?

____

- What number is Teresa making? ▶ The number ☐
- Represent the number Carl will make.

☐☐☐ ☐☐ ☐

Tip

Go back to **Unit 2** to review composing and decomposing numbers.

Let's Learn

Composing a number means constructing a number using the place value of its digits.

2 hundreds, 5 tens and 9 ones → 259

200 + 50 + 9 → 259

Decomposing a number means breaking down a number using the place value of its digits.

862 → 8 hundreds, 6 tens and 2 ones

862 → 800 + 60 + 2

Let's Practice

1. Decompose the numbers. Apply

a.

658

________ hundreds, ________ tens and ________ ones

☐ + ☐ + ☐

b.

962

________ hundreds, ________ tens and ________ ones

☐ + ☐ + ☐

Quiz Yourself

Read the situation and answer.

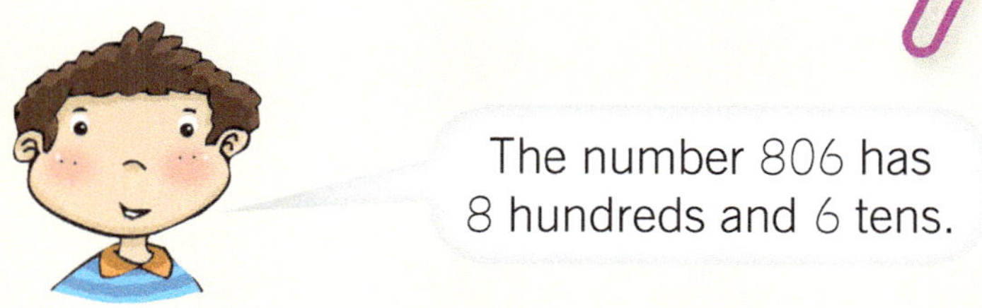

- Is the boy correct?

  (Yes) (No), because ____

  ____.

- Represent the number 806 by completing the number cards.

Let's Check!

Reading and Writing Numbers Up To 1,000

1. Write the word form.

a. 256 ▶ ______________________

b. 650 ▶ ______________________

c. 809 ▶ ______________________

d. 500 ▶ ______________________

Hundreds and Thousands

2. Use **Cutout 4** on **page 159**. Compose and represent the number.

2 hundreds and 6 tens

Counting by 100s Up To 1,000

3. Count by 100s:

a. Count forward. Start with 350.

350, ____, ____, ____, ____

b. Count backward. Start with 952.

952, ____, ____, ____, ____

Place Value

4. Color the numbers where the digit 3 has a place value of 300.

203 130 930

350 643 379 837

Composing and Decomposing Numbers

5. Decompose and compose the numbers.

a. 658 = ____ + ____ + ____

b. 900 + 60 + 9 = ____

How Did You Do?

For each color a .

Strategies for Solving Addition Operations

Let's Connect

Students have collected toys to give away for Christmas. They have collected 245 toys for girls and 233 toys for boys.

Louis and Maggie calculated the number of toys differently.

Louis

$$\begin{array}{rcccc} 245 & = & 200 & 40 & 5 \\ +233 & = & 200 & 30 & 3 \\ \hline & & 400 + & 70 + & 8 = 478 \end{array}$$

We collected 478 toys in total.

Maggie

	H	T	O
	2	4	5
+	2	3	3
	4	7	8

We collected 478 toys in total.

- How did Louis calculate the total number of toys? Explain his strategy.

- How did Maggie calculate the total number of toys? Explain her strategy.

- Did they get the same answer? Why or why not? Explain.

Tip

The terms in an addition operation are:

$$\begin{array}{r} 34 \\ +\ 51 \\ \hline 85 \end{array}$$

34, 51 ▶ addend

85 ▶ sum

Let's Learn

There are different **strategies** you can use to solve **addition** operations.

By **adding in columns:** The ones, tens and hundreds are added without breaking down any number.

	H	T	O
	4	2	1
+	2	3	5
	6	5	6

By **decomposing:** The **addends** are broken down based on the place values of their numbers. Then they are composed.

$421 = 400 \quad 20 \quad 1$

$+235 = 200 \quad 30 \quad 5$

$600 + 50 + 6 = 656$

Let's Practice

1. Solve the addition operations. Apply

a.

	H	T	O
	1	5	0
+	3	2	0

$150 = \square \quad \square \quad \square$

$+320 = \square \quad \square \quad \square$

$\square + \square + \square = \square$

b.

	H	T	O
	2	3	5
+	6	2	4

$235 = \square \quad \square \quad \square$

$+624 = \square \quad \square \quad \square$

$\square + \square + \square = \square$

Strategies for Solving Subtraction Operations

Let's Connect

A class collects 478 toys, and they donate 116 to a kindergarten. Thomas and Maria want to know how many toys are left. They use different strategies.

Thomas

$$\begin{array}{rcl} 478 & = & 400 \quad 70 \quad 8 \\ -\ 116 & = & 100 \quad 10 \quad 6 \\ \hline & & 300 + 60 + 2 = 362 \end{array}$$

There are 362 toys left.

Maria

	H	T	O
	4	7	8
−	1	1	6
	3	6	2

There are 362 toys left.

- How did Thomas calculate the number of toys left? Explain.

____

____

- How did Maria calculate the number of toys left? Explain.

____

____

Tip

The terms in a subtraction operation are:

$$\begin{array}{rl} 56 & \text{minuend} \\ -23 & \text{subtrahend} \\ \hline 33 & \text{difference} \end{array}$$

Education through Values

Would you and your classmates like to start a fundraiser to collect toys and give them to a charity for children?

Let's Learn

There are different **strategies** you can use to solve **subtraction** operations.

By **subtracting in columns:** The ones, tens and hundreds are subtracted without breaking down any number.

	H	T	O
	8	4	5
−	2	3	1
	6	1	4

By **decomposing:** The **minuend** and **subtrahend** are broken down based on the place value of their numbers. Then the subtrahend values are subtracted from the minuend values.

$$845 = 800 \quad 40 \quad 5$$
$$-231 = 200 \quad 30 \quad 1$$
$$600 + 10 + 4 = 614$$

Let's Practice

1. Solve the subtraction operations. Apply

a.

	H	T	O
	5	6	0
−	2	1	0

560 = ☐ ☐ ☐

− 210 = ☐ ☐ ☐

☐ + ☐ + ☐ = ☐

b.

	H	T	O
	9	9	9
−	8	1	8

999 = ☐ ☐ ☐

− 818 = ☐ ☐ ☐

☐ + ☐ + ☐ = ☐

Word Problems with Addition and Subtraction

Let's Connect

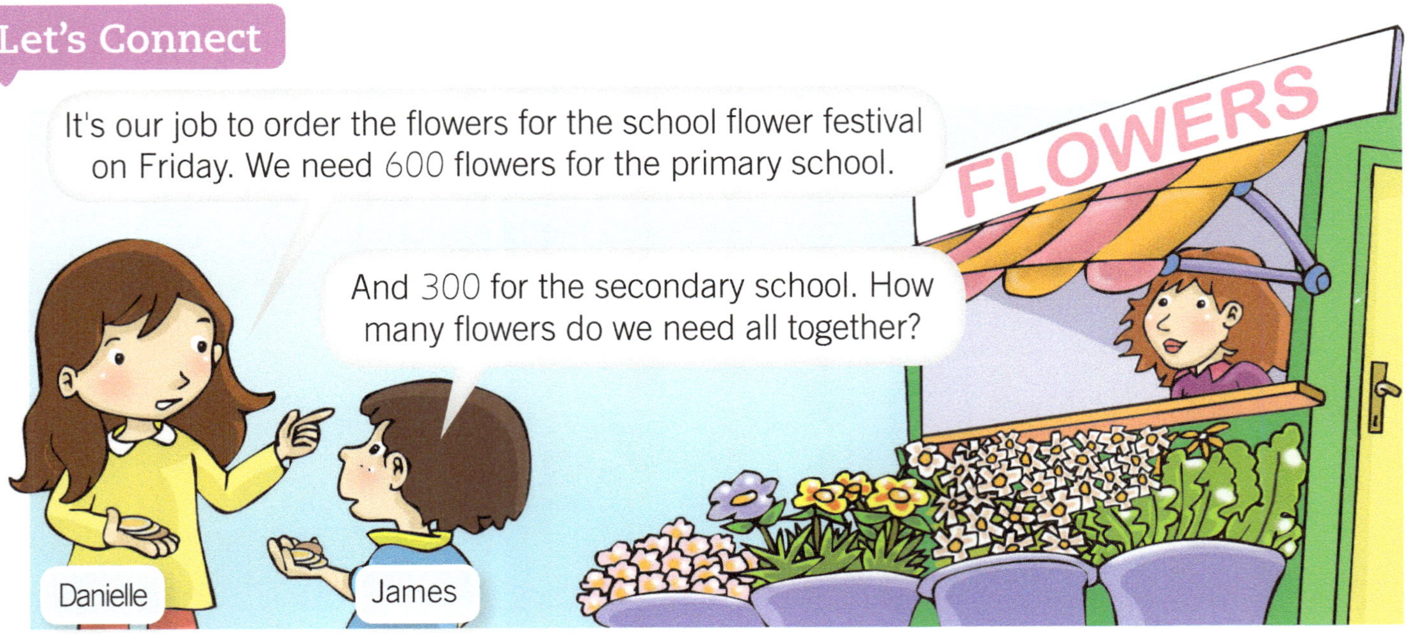

- Explain, in your own words, what James asks Danielle.

____

- What information does Danielle have to answer the question?

____

____

- Which operation will Danielle use to answer the question? Mark the operation and solve it.

☐ addition ☐ subtraction

answer ▶ ________________________________

Let's Learn

A word problem is a math problem about a specific situation that is written out in words.

Read the **situation** and **identify the information** that will answer the **question**.

Danielle and James need 600 flowers for the primary school and 300 for the secondary school.

How many flowers do Danielle and James need?

Choose the correct **operation** and pick a **strategy** to solve the problem.

	H	T	O
	6	0	0
+	3	0	0
	9	0	0

Answer the question.

Danielle and James need 900 flowers in total.

1. Identify the important information from the questions. Mark the operations that solve the word problems with a ✔. Then answer the word problems. Analyze

a. Paulina has $940 and she donates $500 to a charity. How much money does she have left?

information ▶ ______________________

answer ▶ ______________________

☐ addition

☐ subtraction

b. A choir is made up of two groups of people. In one group there are 63 people, and in the other there are 103 people. How many people are in the choir in all?

information ▶ ______________________

answer ▶ ______________________

☐ addition

☐ subtraction

Exam Strategies

Look and Learn

Mark the correct answer with an ✗.

1 How is the number seven hundred eighty written numerically?

- [A] 680
- [B] 708
- [✗C] 780

Read the question carefully.

Find the correct answer in the options and mark it with an ✗.

Your Turn!

Mark the correct answer with an ✗ .

2 What is the word form for 603?

- [A] Sixty-three
- [B] Six hundred three
- [C] Six hundred thirty

What Did You Learn?

Final Evaluation

Reading and Writing Numbers Up To 1,000

1. Write the numbers.

a. Five hundred twelve ▶ ______

b. Two hundred three ▶ ______

c. Three hundred fifty ▶ ______

2. Write the word forms of the numbers.

a. 430 ▶ ______________________

b. 716 ▶ ______________________

c. 188 ▶ ______________________

d. 293 ▶ ______________________

Counting by 100s Up To 1,000

3. Answer the word problems.

a.

Count forward by 100s and start with 251. What is the third number?

The third number is ______.

b.

When counting backward by 100s starting with 698, what is the fifth number?

The fifth number is ______.

Composing and Decomposing Numbers

4. Compose and decompose the numbers.

a. 506 = ☐ + ☐ + ☐

b. 900 + 20 + 7 = ☐

c. 472 = ☐ + ☐ + ☐

d. 500 + 0 + 5 = ☐

Addition and Subtraction Word Problems

5. An animal adoption center has 210 dogs and 89 cats. How many animals are at the adoption center in all?

information ▶ ______________________

____

☐ addition

☐ subtraction

strategy

answer ▶ ______________________

Mark the correct answer with an ✕.

Use the picture to answer <u>questions 6 and 7.</u>

6. Michael goes to the store with $251. How many hundreds, tens and ones does he have?

A	2	0	0	5	0	1
B	5	0	0	1	0	2
C	1	0	0	2	0	5

7. Michael has $251. He buys chocolate milk, strawberry milk and yogurt with cereal. How much money does he have left?

A $227

B $230

C $231

Find Test 4 Study Page

How Did You Do?

For each ☺ color a ⬭.

Unit 5

Multiplication and Number Sequences

Key Words

multiplication

$3 \times 6 = 18$

times

$\times$

repeated addition

$3 + 3 + 3 + 3$

number sequence

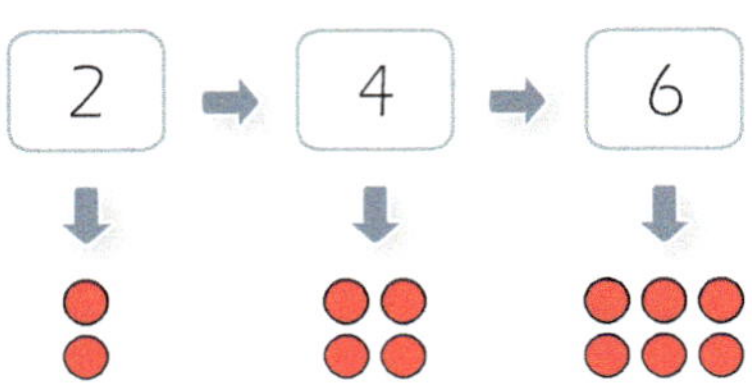

In this unit you will learn to:

- count by 2s, 5s and 10s and understand their relation to multiplication.
- understand simple representations of multiplication.
- understand multiplication as repeated addition.
- recognize, continue and complete number sequences.
- do your work in a clear and organized way.

What Do You Know? Initial Evaluation

Look at the picture and answer.

1. How many groups of  are there?

   There are ☐ groups.

2. How many  does each group have?

   Each group has ☐ .

3. How many  are there in the four tanks on the left?

   There are ☐ in total.

4. How many  are there in the four tanks on the left?

   There are ☐ in total.

5. Draw two groups of 7  in the empty fish tanks.

   starfish

Section 1 Math Strategies

Counting by 2s

Let's Connect

Andrea and Jim are playing a guessing game.

- How many shoes does one person wear? Represent the shoes using ●.

I count ___ shoes.

- How many shoes do two people wear? Represent the shoes using ●.

I count ___ shoes.

- How many more shoes do you count each time a person is added? I count ___ shoes.

- What numbers will Jim count?

2, ___, ___, ___, ___, ___, ___, ___, ___, ___

Let's Learn

When **counting by 2s,** you add or subtract 2 each time.

When counting **forward** by 2s:

2, 4, 6, 8, 10, 12, 14 — add 2

When counting **backward** by 2s:

20, 18, 16, 14, 12, 10, 8 — subtract 2

Let's Practice

1. Count by 2s to complete the number series. Apply

a. 12, 14, 16, 18, ___, ___

b. 92, 90, 88, 86, ___, ___

c. 52, 54, 56, 58, ___, ___

Challenge

"2, 4, 6, 8 who do we appreciate? Teacher! Teacher! Goooo Teacher!" Now choose a friend and chant for them, too!

2. Count by 2s to complete the number series. Apply

a. Start with 28 and count forward.

28, ___, ___, ___, ___, ___, ___

b. Start with 58 and count backward.

58, ___, ___, ___, ___, ___, ___

Counting by 5s

Let's Connect

Carla's uniform includes a sweater with 5 buttons.

- How many buttons can you count on each student's sweater? Represent them using ●.

I count ☐ buttons.

- How many buttons can you count on two students' sweaters? Represent them using ●.

I count ☐ buttons.

- How many buttons can you count on three students' sweaters? Represent them using ●.

I count ☐ buttons.

- How many more buttons do you count each time you add a student? I count ☐ buttons.

- What numbers will Carla count?

5, ☐, ☐, ☐, ☐, ☐, ☐, ☐, ☐, ☐

Let's Learn

When **counting by 5s**, you add or subtract 5 each time.

When counting **forward** by 5s:

5, 10, 15, 20, 25, 30, 35 — add 5

When counting **backward** by 5s:

50, 45, 40, 35, 30, 25, 20 — subtract 5

Let's Practice

1. Count the number sequences. Trace forward or backward. Identify

a. 15, 20, 25, 30, 35, 40 — forward — backward

b. 90, 85, 80, 75, 70, 65 — forward — backward

2. Complete by counting by 5s forward or backward. Apply

a. 20, 25, 30, 35, ____, ____

b. 80, 75, 70, 65, ____, ____

3. Complete by counting by 5s. Start with 85 and count backward.

85, ____, ____, ____, ____, ____, ____

Challenge

Around the World
The first person starts with 5, then the next person counts by 5 and says 10, and so on. The first person to make a mistake is out. How high can you go?

Counting by 10s

Let's Connect

- How many notebooks are in two packs? Represent them using ●.

I count ___ notebooks.

- How many notebooks are in 3 packs? There are ___ notebooks in 3 packs.

- How many notebooks are in 10 packs? Complete by adding the number of notebooks in each pack.

10, ___, ___, ___, ___, ___, ___, ___, ___, ___

Let's Learn

When **counting by 10s**, you add or subtract 10 each time.

When counting **forward** by 10s:

10, 20, 30, 40, 50, 60, 70 — add 10

When counting **backward** by 10s:

100, 90, 80, 70, 60, 50, 40 — subtract 10

Let's Practice

1. Count by 10s. Apply

a. Start with 30 and count forward.

30, ____, ____, ____, ____, ____, ____

b. Start with 90 and count backward.

90, ____, ____, ____, ____, ____, ____

Quiz Yourself

Look at how the children count and answer.

- What numbers are the children counting by? Explain.

____

____

Section 2
Representing Multiplication

Groups with Equal Numbers of Objects

Let's Connect

Peter is storing his toy car collection in boxes.

- How many boxes did Peter use to store his cars? He used ☐ boxes.
- How many cars did he store in each box? Represent the cars using **Cutout 5** on **page 161**.

Peter stored ☐ cars in each box.

- How many equal groups of cars are there? There are ☐ groups of ☐ cars.

Education through Values

If you keep your toys and materials well organized, you can find them faster and keep your house and classroom clean and tidy.

Let's Learn

Multiplication is related to counting equal groups of objects.
How many pencils are there?

There are 2 pencil cases.
Each pencil case has 3 pencils.

There are 2 **times** 3 pencils.

$2 \times 3 = 6$

Let's Practice

1. Look at the pictures. Complete. Apply

a.

There are ___ trays.

Each tray has ___ glasses.

There are ___ times ___ glasses.

b.

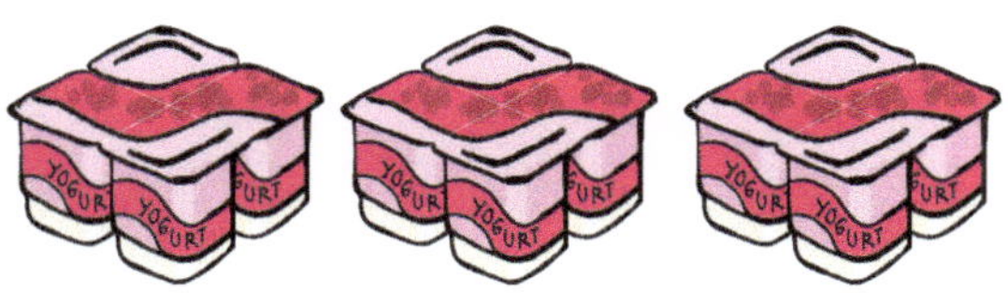

There are ___ packs of yogurt.

Each pack has ___ cups of yogurt.

There are ___ times ___ cups of yogurt.

2. Draw the group of objects. Complete. Represent

There are 2 bags each with 10 nuts.

There are ___ times ___ nuts.

Multiplication as Repeated Addition

Let's Connect

- How many eggs are in each carton?

There are ☐ eggs in each of the ☐ cartons.

- Represent the quantity of eggs in each carton using **Cutout 6** on **page 161**.

- The lady adds the number of eggs in each carton in order to know how many eggs she is buying in total. How many eggs are there? Complete the addition operation.

carton 1		carton 2		carton 3		total number of eggs
☐	+	☐	+	☐	=	☐

Let's Learn

Multiplication can be expressed as the addition of the same number, or **repeated addition**.

The symbol for **multiplication** is × and we read it as "**times.**"

6 + 6 + 6 = 18

There are 3 fishbowls, each with 6 fish.

3 **times** 6 fish can be expressed as:

$$3 \times 6 = 18$$

There are a total of 18 fish.

Let's Practice

1. Count the objects and complete. Interpret

a.

☐ + ☐ + ☐ + ☐

There are ☐ times ☐ flowers.

b.

☐ + ☐ + ☐

There are ☐ times ☐ ladybugs.

2. Write each addition operation as a multiplication operation. Apply

a. $3 + 3 + 3 + 3 + 3 + 3$

☐ times ☐

☐ × ☐

c. $1 + 1 + 1 + 1 + 1 + 1 + 1 + 1$

☐ times ☐

☐ × ☐

b. $6 + 6 + 6 + 6 + 6$

☐ times ☐

☐ × ☐

d. $8 + 8 + 8 + 8 + 8 + 8$

☐ times ☐

☐ × ☐

3. Represent the multiplication situations using ●. Apply

a. Pamela has 4 bags with 9 apples in each.

b. Peter has 6 bags with 8 pears in each.

4. Write the answer for each multiplication using a repeated addition. Apply

a. 4×3

☐ + ☐ + ☐ + ☐ = ☐

b. 2×6

☐ + ☐ = ☐

c. 5×8

☐ + ☐ + ☐ + ☐ + ☐ = ☐

d. 3×7

☐ + ☐ + ☐ = ☐

Quiz Yourself

Read the problem. Use Cutout 7 on page 161 to represent the situation.

Michelle's mother will bake some oatmeal cookies. Michelle wants to make 5 bags with 4 cookies each to give to her friends. How many cookies should her mother make?

Answer: ______________________________

Let's Check!

Counting by 2s, 5s and 10s

1. Complete the number series.

a. Start with 18, then count forward by 2s.

18, ___, ___, ___, ___, ___, ___

b. Start with 75, then count backward by 5s.

75, ___, ___, ___, ___, ___, ___

c. Start with 90, then count backward by 10s.

90, ___, ___, ___, ___, ___, ___

Groups with Equal Numbers of Objects

2. Use the pictures to answer.

a.

There are ___ fishbowls.

Each fishbowl has ___ fish.

There are ___ times ___ fish.

b.

There are ___ sweaters.

Each sweater has ___ buttons.

There are ___ times ___ buttons.

3. Match each picture with its description.

a.

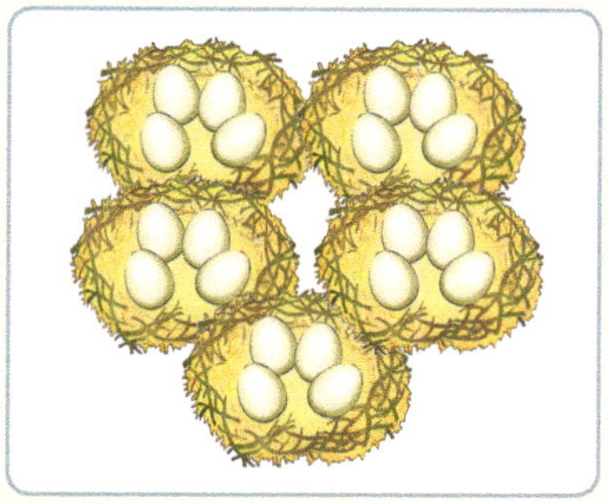

b.

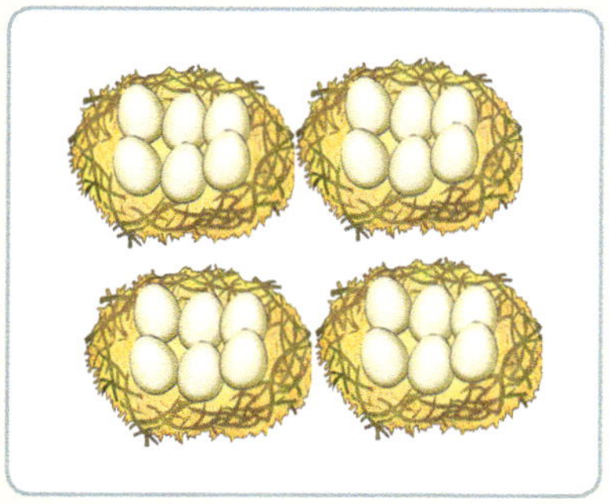

c.

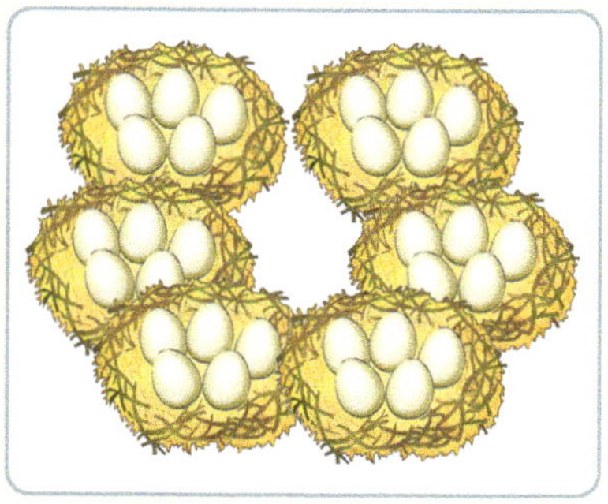

There are 6 groups of 5 eggs.

There are 5 groups of 4 eggs.

There are 4 groups of 6 eggs.

Multiplication as Repeated Addition

4. Write each addition operation as a multiplication operation and answer.

a. 7 + 7 + 7

☐ times ☐

☐ × ☐ = ☐

b. 6 + 6 + 6 + 6

☐ times ☐

☐ × ☐ = ☐

How Did You Do?

For each (frog face) color a (lily pad).

Representing Number Sequences

Let's Connect

Nina builds a tower with 8 blocks using the pattern:

Start with 2 blocks and add 2 each time.

2 → 4 → 6 → 8

1

2

3

4

- How many blocks does Nina's tower have?

picture 1	picture 2	picture 3	picture 4
↓	↓	↓	↓

Remember!

The **pattern** of a sequence is the rule that says how the things in the sequence are arranged.

- Did Nina represent the sequence correctly? Explain.

Yes No, because ______________________________.

Let's Learn

We can use **objects** or **symbols** to represent a number sequence.

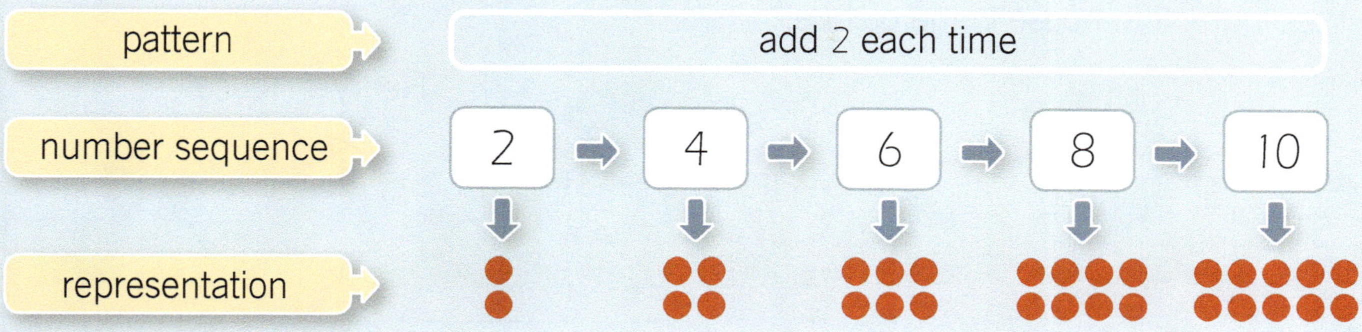

Let's Practice

1. Use **Cutout 8** on **page 163** to represent the number sequences and write the numbers. Apply

pattern ▶ Remove 3 cubes each time.

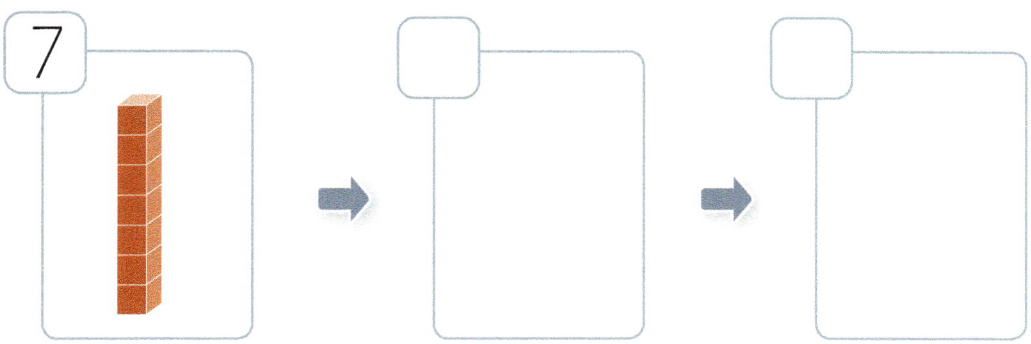

pattern ▶ Add a ⬢ above the line and remove a ⬢ below.

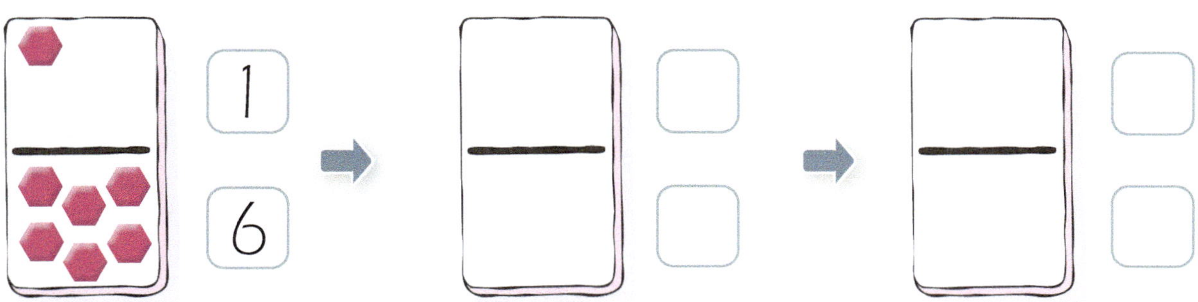

Continuing Number Sequences

Let's Connect

Henry lives in the fifth house in the picture.

- Do the house numbers increase (↑) or decrease (↓)?

____

- What are the house numbers of the first and second houses?

first house ▶ ☐ second house ▶ ☐

- What is the difference between 51 and 47? ☐

- Is the difference between the third and fourth house the same as the difference between the first and second? Explain.

(Yes) (No), because ______________________________.

- What is the house number of the fifth house? Complete.

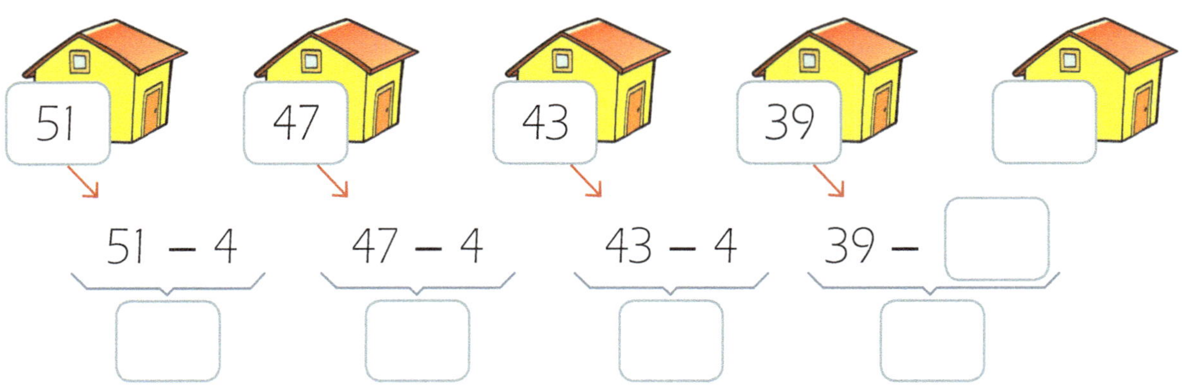

Fun Fact!

Streets are usually separated into even (2,4,6,8, ...) and odd (1,3,5,7, ...) numbers. One side has even house numbers and the other side has odd house numbers.

Let's Learn

To continue a **number sequence** we need to know the **pattern** of the sequence. The pattern tells us how much the sequence increases (↑) by or decreases (↓) by each time.

+ 5 + 5 + 5

70 → 75 → 80 → 85

increase ▸ add 5

− 5 − 5 − 5

85 → 80 → 75 → 70

decrease ▸ subtract 5

Let's Practice

1. Use the patterns to continue the number sequences. Apply

a. pattern ▸ add 7

20 → 27 → ☐ → ☐ → ☐ → ☐ → ☐ → ☐

b. pattern ▸ subtract 3

84 → 81 → ☐ → ☐ → ☐ → ☐ → ☐ → ☐

2. Find the pattern for the sequence. Write the number on the last shirt. Analyze

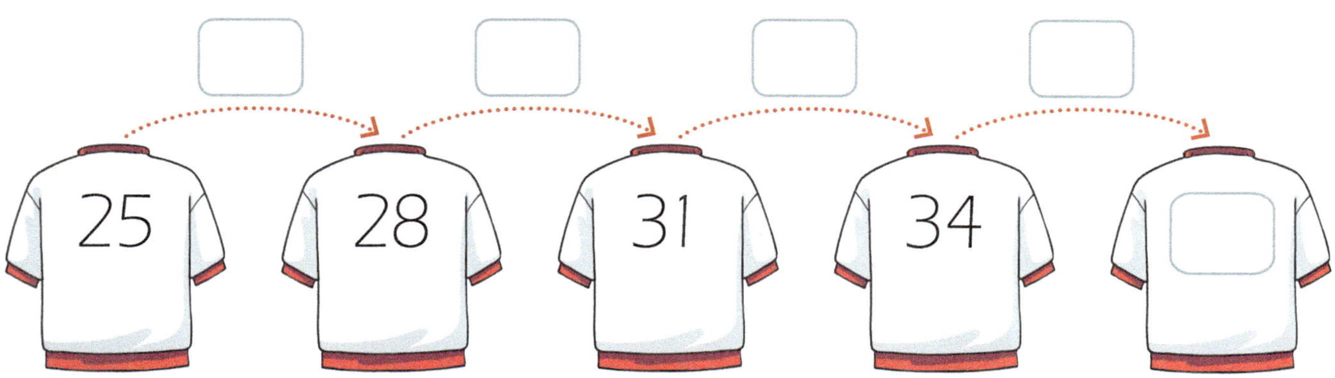

The pattern is ______________________.

Completing Number Sequences

Let's Connect

Ashley has chosen a book and she reads a few pages every day.

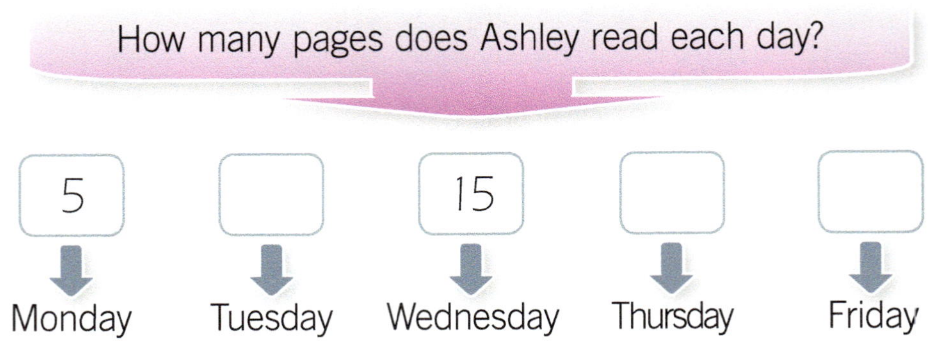

- Ashley reads 5 pages on Monday and will read a total of 10 pages by Tuesday night. How many pages will she read on Tuesday?

  On Tuesday, Ashley will read ☐ pages.

- Ashley will read a total of 15 pages of her book by Wednesday night. How many pages will she read on Wednesday?

  On Wednesday, Ashley will read ☐ pages.

- How many pages will Ashley read every day?

  Ashley will read ☐ pages every day.

- Does the total number of pages Ashley reads increase or decrease?

  ___

- How many pages will Ashley read by Friday night? ☐ → Friday

Let's Learn

To **complete** a number sequence, you need to **identify** the **pattern**.

4 → 8 → 12 → ☐ → 20 → ☐

In this number sequence the pattern is **add 4**.

+ 4, + 4, + 4, + 4, + 4

4 → 8 → 12 → 16 → 20 → 24

Let's Practice

1. Use the pattern to complete the number sequence. Apply

pattern ▶ subtract 4

72 → ☐ → 64 → 60 → ☐ → ☐ → 48 → ☐

2. Mark the correct patterns with a ✔. Identify

a. The pattern is: ☐ add 6 ☐ add 8

18 → 24 → ☐ → 36 → 42 → ☐ → 54

b. The pattern is: ☐ subtract 10 ☐ add 10

1 → 11 → 21 → ☐ → ☐ → 51 → 61

Exam Strategies

Look and Learn

Mark the correct answer with an ✖.

1 Which picture represents 4×3?

A 

B 

C 

Read the word problem carefully. Look at the choices and decide which one represents 4×3.

Look for your answer and mark it with an ✖.

Your Turn!

Mark the correct answer with an ✖.

2 Which picture represents 5×2?

A 

B 

C 

What Did You Learn?

Final Evaluation

Groups with Equal Numbers of Objects

1. Use the pictures to complete the sentences.

a.

There are ____ groups of chicks.

Each group has ____ chicks.

There are ____ times ____ chicks.

b.

There are ____ mail boxes.

Each mail box has ____ letters.

There are ____ times ____ letters.

Multiplication as Repeated Addition

2. Write the addition operations as multiplication operations. Represent the operations with drawings.

a. $9 + 9 + 9$

____ × ____ = ____

b. $4 + 4 + 4 + 4 + 4$

____ × ____ = ____

Continuing Number Sequences

3. Use the patterns to complete the number sequences.

a. pattern ▶ add 6

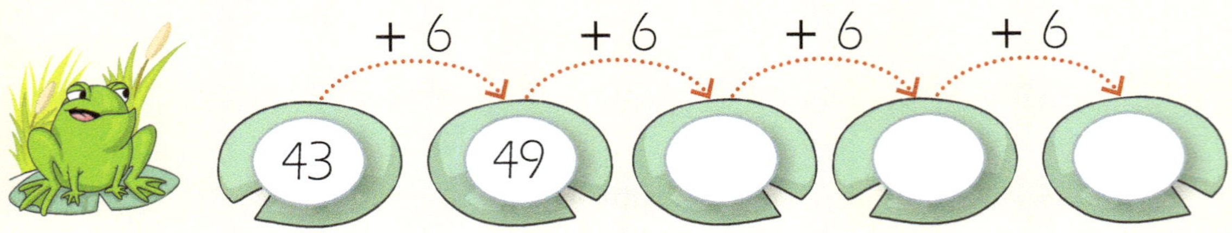

b. pattern ▶ subtract 11

Completing Number Sequences

4. Find and write the patterns. Write the numbers in the number sequences.

a. pattern ▶ ____________________.

b. pattern ▶ ____________________.

Mark the correct answer with an ✗.

5. Which answer represents 2 × 3?

A 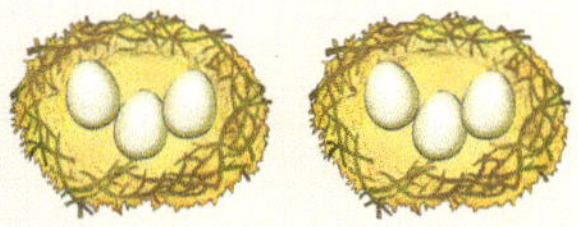

B 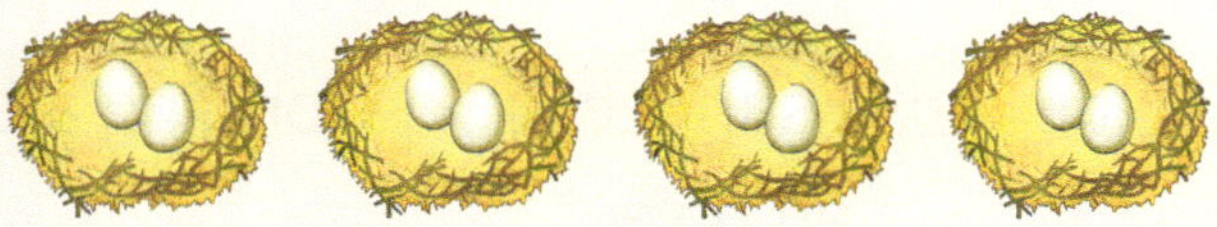

C 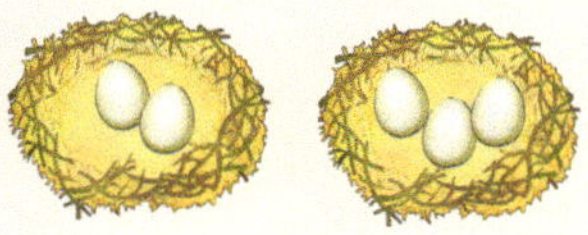

6. A truck has 5 baskets with 8 apples in each. How many apples are there in all?

A 13 apples

B 40 apples

C 80 apples

7. What is the pattern for this number sequence?

80	65	50	35	20	5

A Add 15

B Subtract 15

C Subtract 10

Find Test 5 Study Page

How Did You Do?

For each 🐸 color a ⬭.

Glossary

2.1 Key Words Unit 1

decreasing – *adj*, becoming smaller in size, amount, number, etc.

equal – *adj*, having the same mathematical value

increasing – *adj*, becoming larger or greater in size, amount, number, etc.

pattern – *n*, the regular and repeated way in which something happens or is done

2.2 Key Words Unit 2

estimate – *v*, to form a general idea about the value, size or cost of something

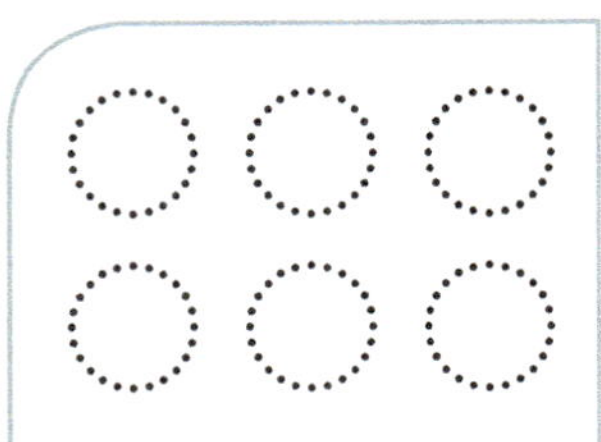

hundreds – *n*, the place value third from the right that represents groups of 100s

ones – *n*, the place value farthest to the right that represents 1s

place value – *n*, the value assigned to a digit within a number, based on its location in that number

tens – *n*, the place value second from the right that represents groups of 10s

2.3 Key Words Unit 3

on – *prep*, used to indicate position in contact with and supported by the top surface of something

side – *n*, a surface or line forming a border or face of an object

two-dimensional shape – *n*, a shape that has only two dimensions (such as length and width)

under – *prep*, in or to a lower place than something

vertex – *n*, the point where two lines meet to form an angle

2.4 Key Words Unit 4

adding in columns – *phr*, a strategy for solving an addition without breaking down any numbers

compose – *v*, to form a number by adding its parts

decompose – *v*, to separate a number into its parts

digit – *n*, any of the numerals from 0 to 9

2.5 Key Words Unit 5

multiplication – *n*, an operation of adding a number to itself one or more times

number sequence – *n*, a set of numbers or objects arranged according to a specific rule or pattern

repeated addition – *n*, adding a number to itself one or more times

times – *prep*, multiplied by

A

add – *v*, to put two or more numbers together to find a total or sum

addend – *n*, a number that is added to another

addition – *n*, the act, process or operation of adding

airplane – *n*, a machine that has wings and an engine and that flies through the air

B

backward – *adv*, toward the back or the beginning

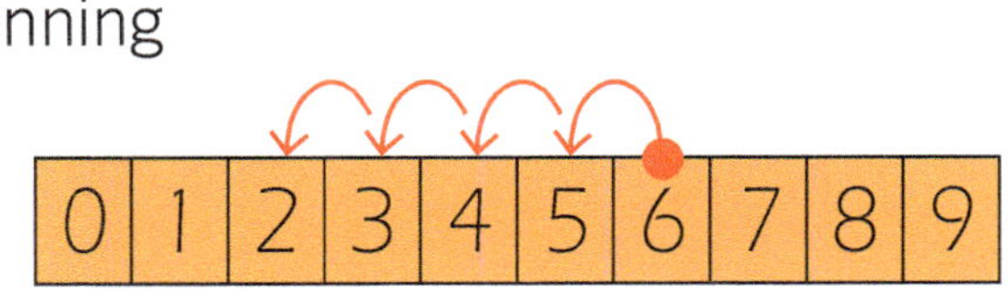

balance – *v*, to arrange so that one set of elements exactly equals another

barn – *n*, a building used for storing grain and hay and for keeping farm animals or farm equipment in

behind – *prep*, at, to or toward the back of

block charts – *n*, information in a graph in the form of blocks

C

calendar – *n*, a chart showing the days, weeks and months of a year

cat – *n*, a small animal that is related to lions and tigers and that is often kept by people as a pet

characteristic – *n*, a special quality or trait that makes a person, thing or group different from others

chick – *n*, a baby bird

collect – *v*, to get (things) from different places and bring them together

count – *v*, to add (people or things) together to find the total number

cow – *n*, a large animal that is raised by people for milk or meat, usually on a farm

D

date – *n*, a particular day of a month or year

day – *n*, a period of 24 hours beginning at midnight

M	T	W	T	F	S	S
Monday	Tuesday	Wednesday	Thursday	Friday	Saturday	Sunday

difference – *n*, the result after subtracting one number from another

dog – *n*, a domestic mammal that eats meat and is closely related to the gray wolf

duck – *n*, a web-footed swimming bird

duckling – *n*, a young duck

E

equal – *adj*, the same in number, amount, degree, rank or quality

equality – *n*, having the same quantity, size or measurement

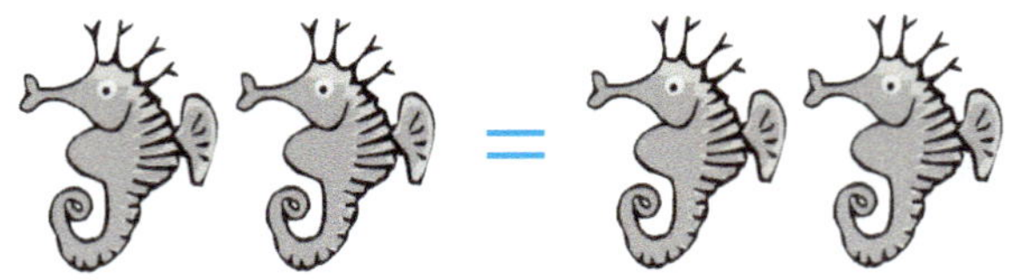

F

fish – *n*, a cold-blooded animal that lives in water

fishbowl – *n*, a glass bowl used for keeping live fish as pets

fish tank – *n*, a glass container in which living water animals and plants are kept

floor – *n*, the part of a room on which you stand

fold – *v*, to bend one part of (something) over or against another part

forward – *adv*, toward the front or end

H

hen – *n*, an adult female chicken

I

imbalanced – *adj*, the state of being out of balance or out of proportion

inequality – *n*, a condition where two quantities are not equal

inside – *prep*, in or into the interior of

interpret – *v*, to explain the meaning of

L

leave (left) – *v*, to have as a remainder

length – *n*, a measurement of how long something is

less – *adj*, smaller in amount or number

M

measure – *v*, to find out the size, length or amount of (something)

measurement – *n*, a size, length or amount known by measuring something

minuend – *n*, a number from which another number is subtracted

month – *n*, one of the twelve parts into which the year is divided

N

number series – *n*, numbers arranged in order following a specific pattern

O

on – *prep*, in contact with and supported by

P

pack – *n*, a group of items packaged as a unit

paint – *n*, a liquid mixture of coloring matter to spread on a surface

paint brush – *n*, a tool used for painting

plant – *n*, a living thing that grows in the ground, usually has leaves or flowers, and needs sun and water to survive

R

record – *v*, to write (something) down so that it can be used or seen again in the future

recycle – *v*, to make something new from something that has been used before

robot – *n*, a real or imaginary machine that looks like a person or an animal controlled by a computer

S

same – *adj*, exactly like someone or something else

scale – *n*, a device that is used for weighing people or things

sea horse – *n*, a small fish that has a head that looks like a horse's head and that swims with its head above its body and tail

sequence – *n*, a group of things that come one after the other

shape – *n*, the form or outline of an object

sheep – *n*, an animal with a thick woolly coat that is often raised for meat or for its wool and skin

shelf – *n*, a flat piece of wood on a wall or in a bookcase to hold objects

similarity – *n*, a point in which things are similar

soccer ball – *n*, a round object used for playing soccer

star fish – *n*, a sea animal that has five arms and that looks like a star

strategy – *n*, a carefully planned way of doing something

subtract – *v*, to take one quantity or number away from another to find the remainder

subtrahend – *n*, a number that is subtracted from another number

survey – *n*, an activity in which many people are asked questions in order to gather information about what most people do or think about something

T

table – *n*, an orderly arrangement of facts or figures in rows or columns for quick reference

tally – *n*, a score or point made

trough – *n*, a long shallow container for the drinking water or feed of domestic animals

U

under – *prep*, below or covered by something

W

week – *n*, a period of seven days

width – *n*, a measurement of how wide something is

window – *n*, an opening in a wall for letting in light or air

Y

yarn – *n*, a long, thin piece of cotton, wool, etc., that is thicker than thread and that is used for knitting and weaving

year – *n*, the regular period of twelve months that begins in January and ends in December

Place Value Chart

Example: 864

H (hundreds)	T (tens)	O (ones)
8	6	4

Math Symbols

Addition	+
Subtraction	−
Equal	=
Multiplication	×

Cutouts

Cutout 1

Use on page 73 (**Unit 3**).

Cutout 2

Use on page 83 (**Unit 3**).

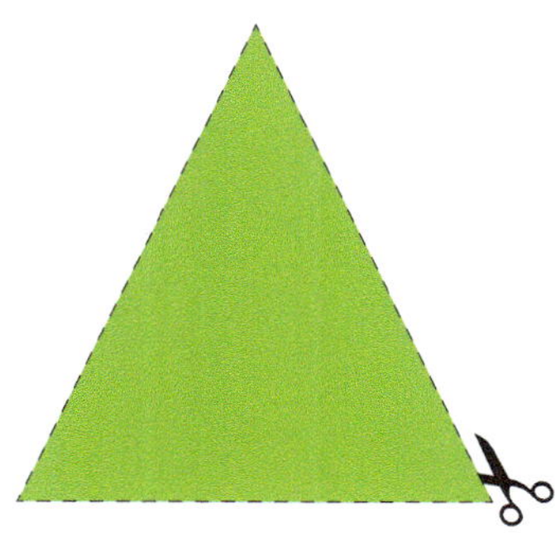

Cutout 3

Use on page 105 (**Unit 4**).

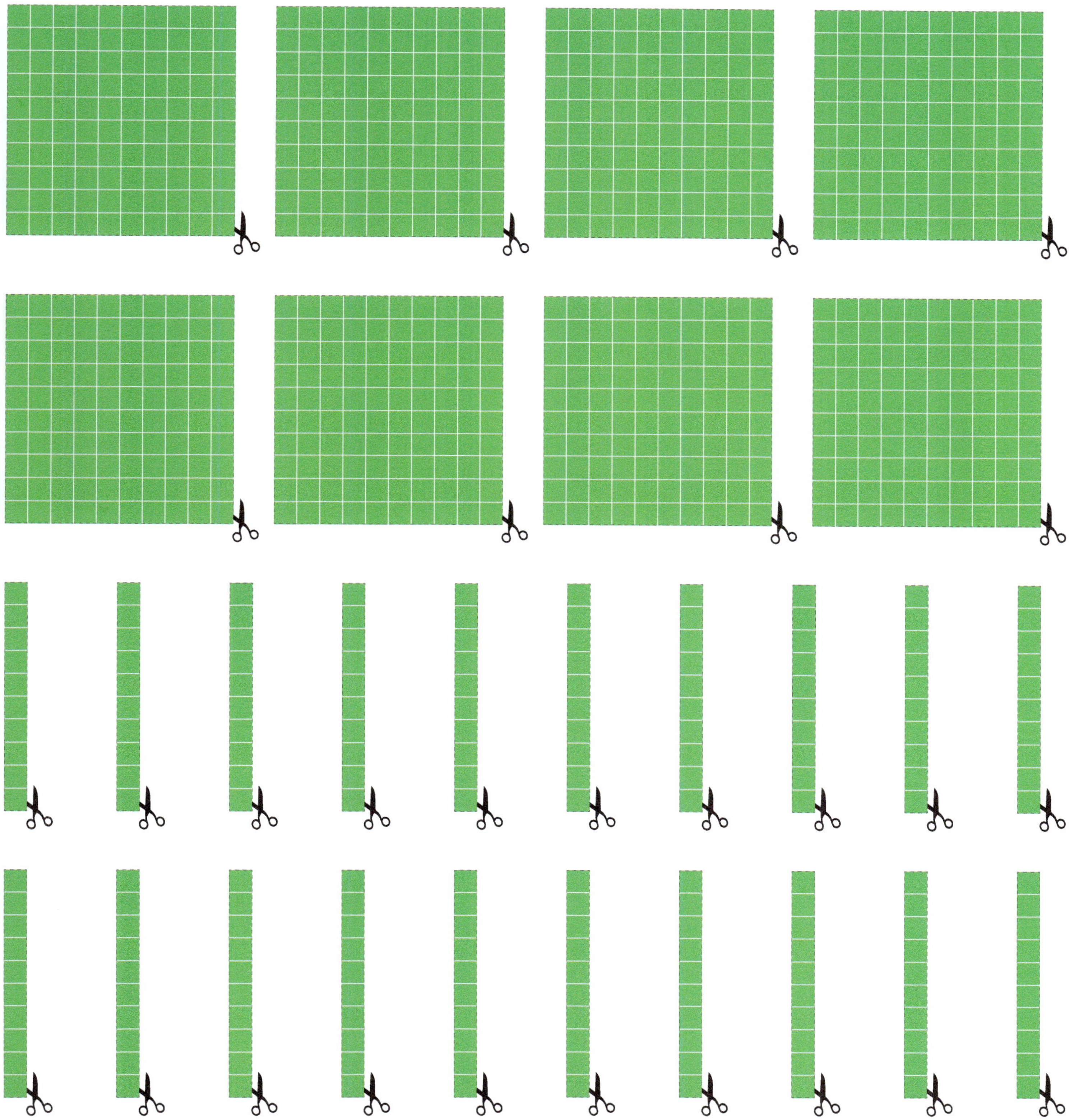

Cutout 4

Use on page 110 (**Unit 4**).

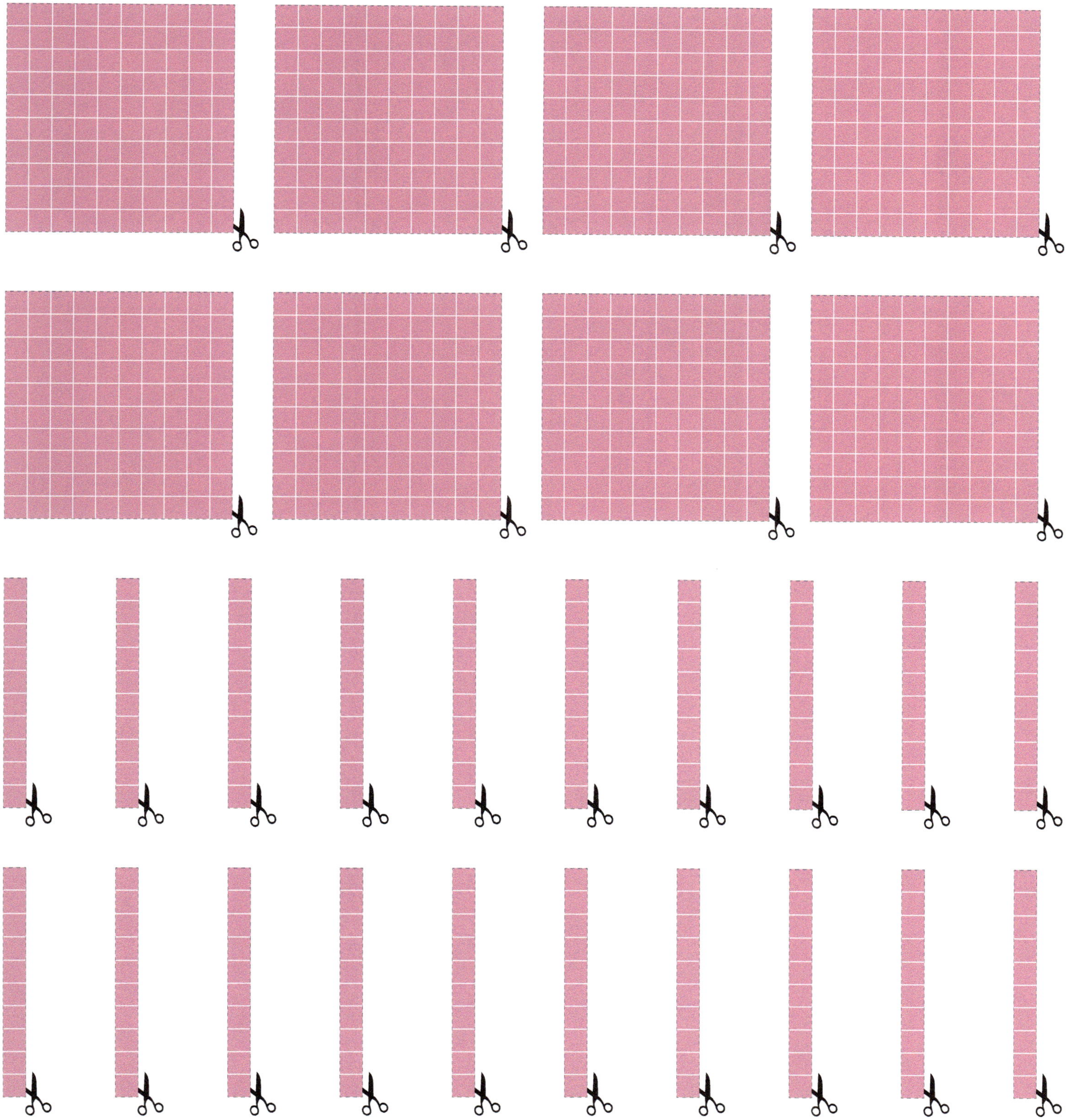

Cutouts

Cutout 5. Use on page 130 (**Unit 5**).

Cutout 6. Use on page 132 (**Unit 5**).

Cutout 7. Use on page 135 (**Unit 5**).

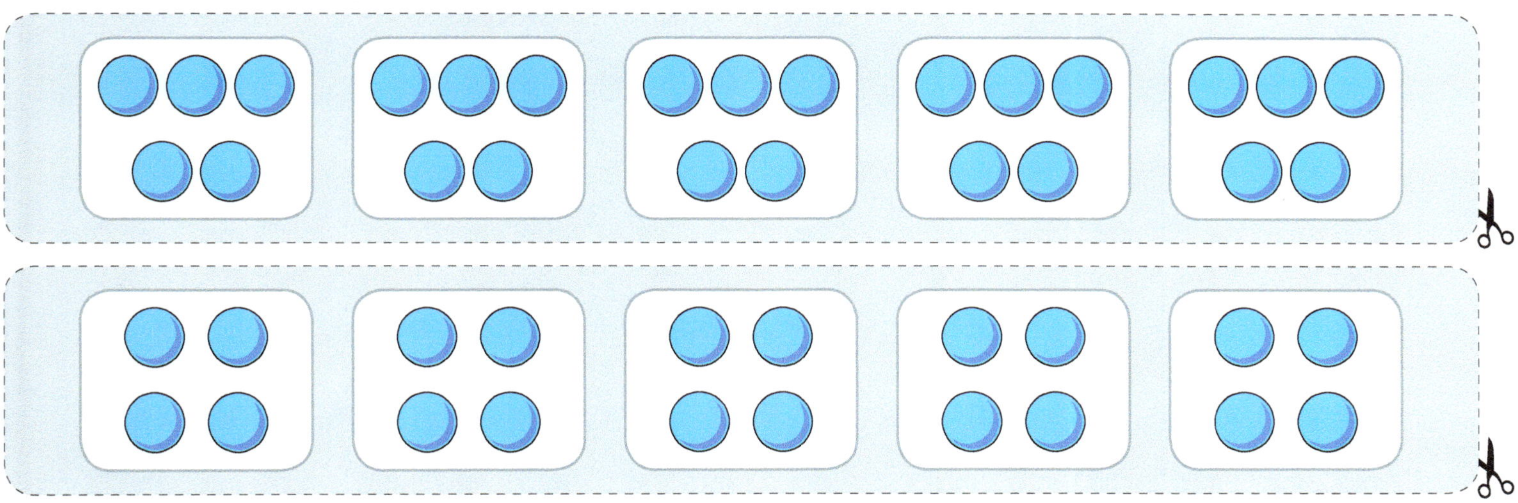

Cutout 8

Use on page 139 (**Unit 5**).

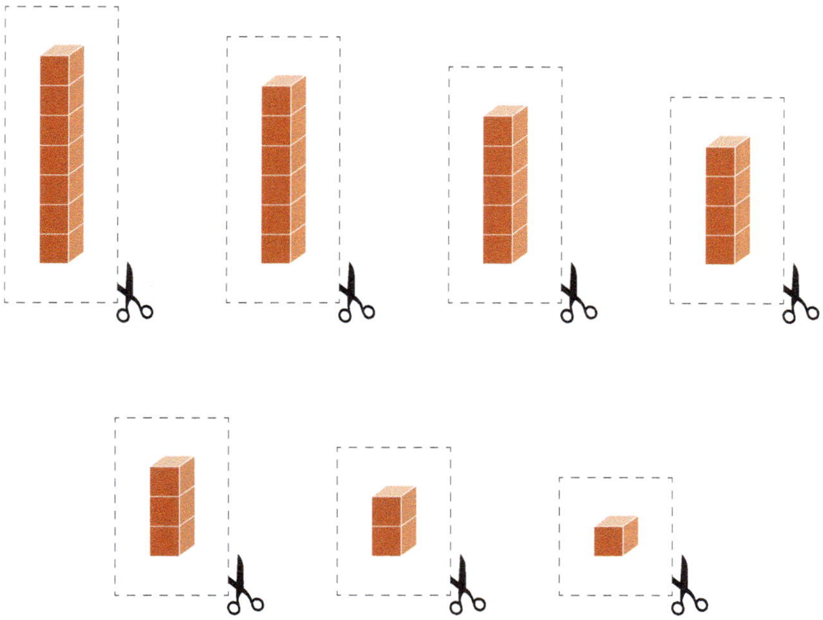

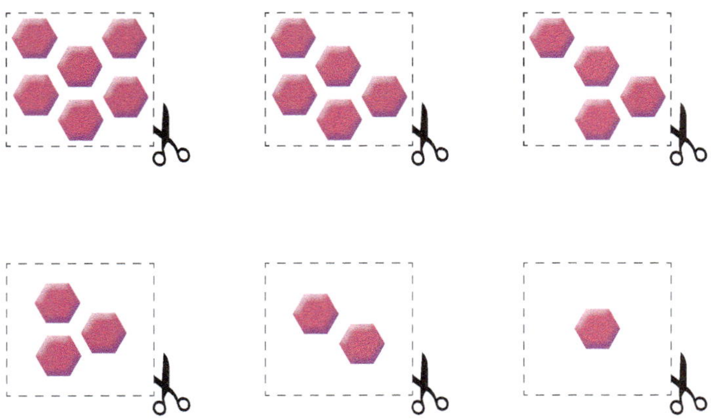

Stickers

Sticker Set 1

Use on page 10 (**Unit 1**).

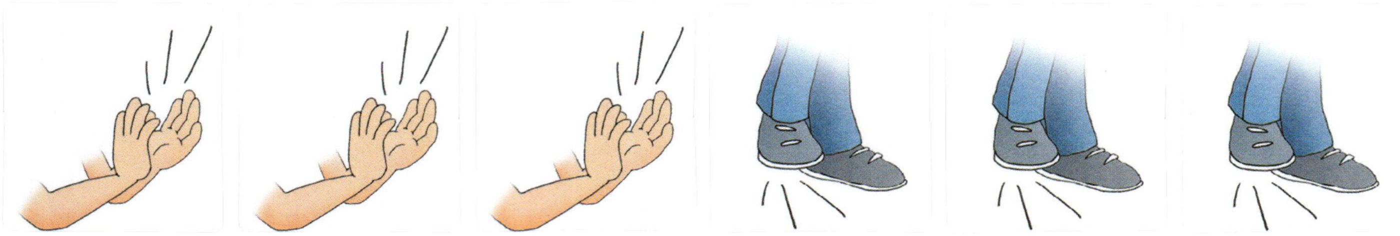

Sticker Set 2

Use on page 13 (**Unit 1**).

a.

b.

c.

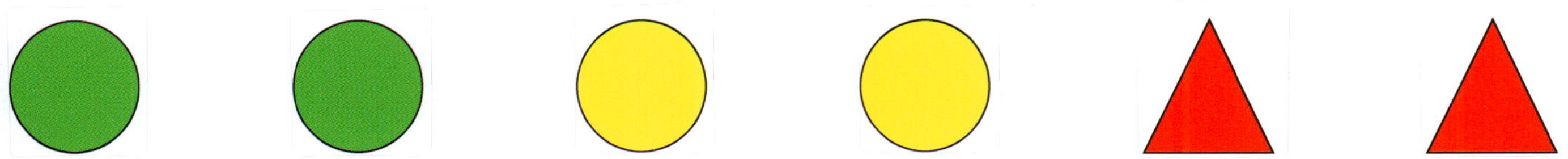

Stickers

Sticker Set 3

Use on page 13 (**Unit 1**).

a.

b.

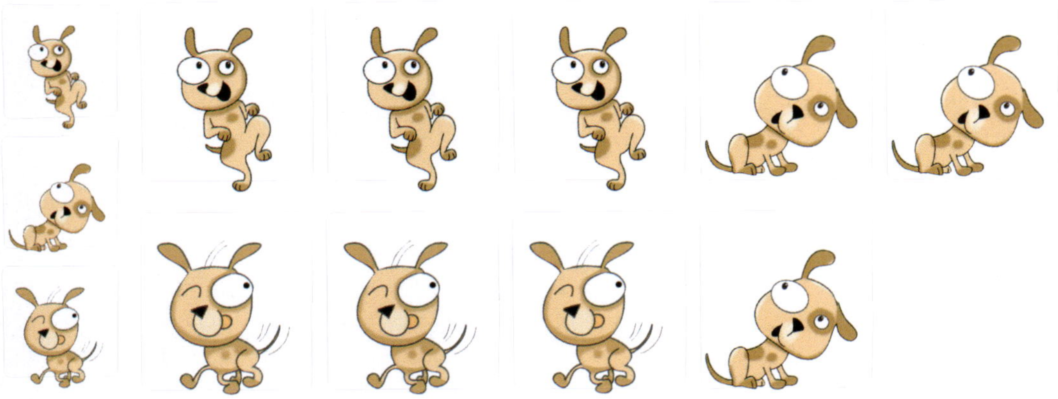

Sticker Set 4

Use on page 16 (**Unit 1**).

a.

b.

Sticker Set 5

Use on page 20 (**Unit 1**).

a.

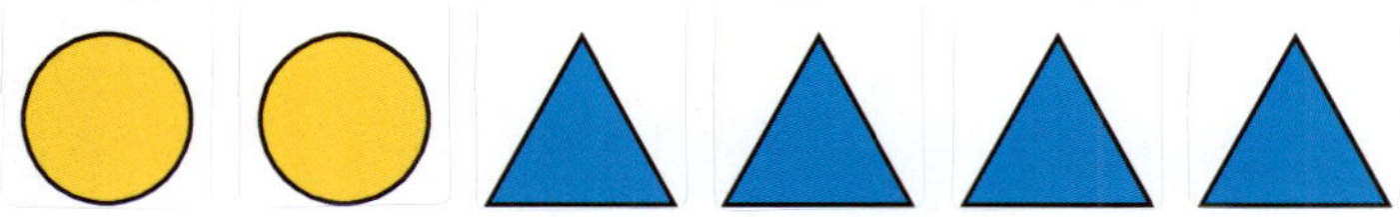

b.

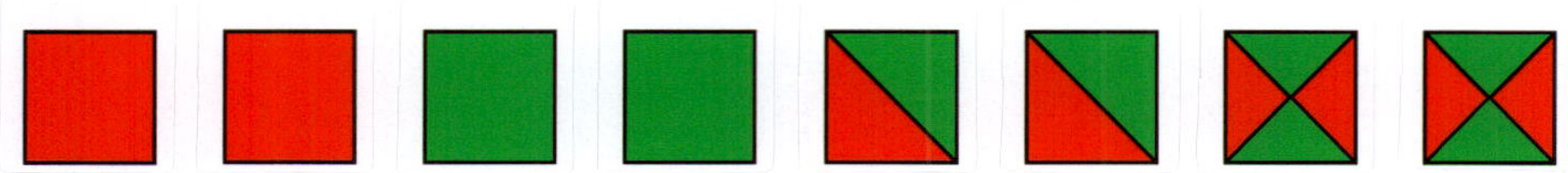

c.

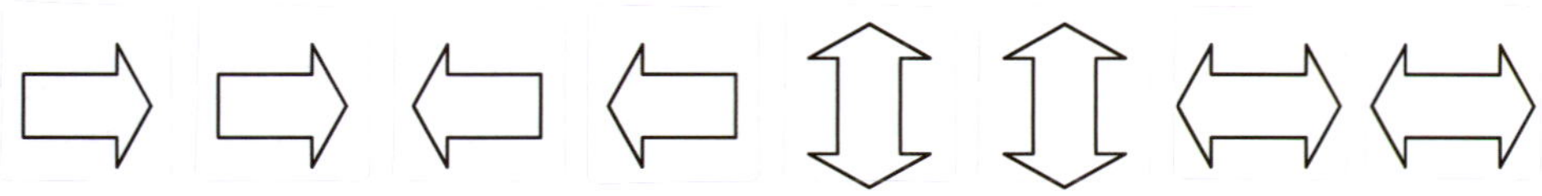

Sticker Set 6

Use on page 28 (**Unit 1**).

a.

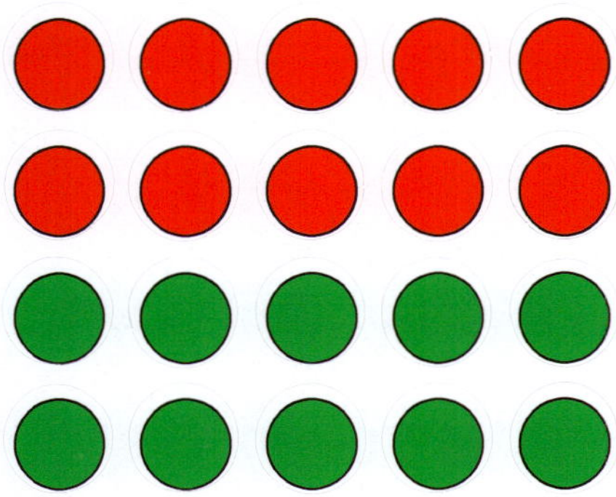

b.

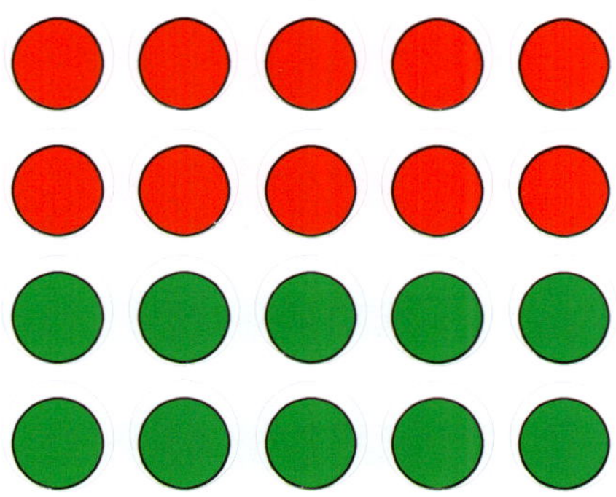

Sticker Set 7

Use on page 30 (**Unit 1**).

Stickers

Sticker Set 8
Use on page 37 (**Unit 2**).

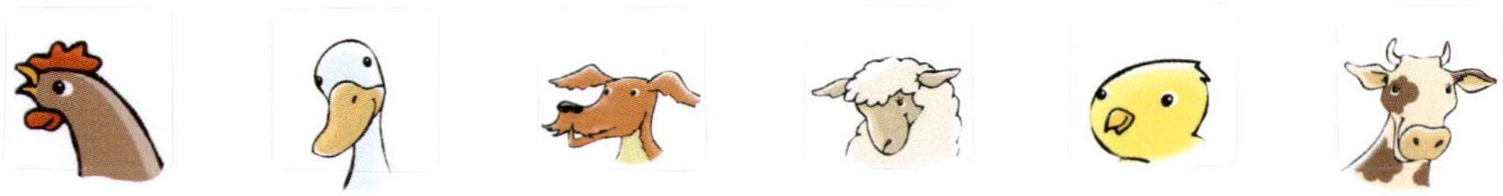

Sticker Set 9
Use on page 42 (**Unit 2**).

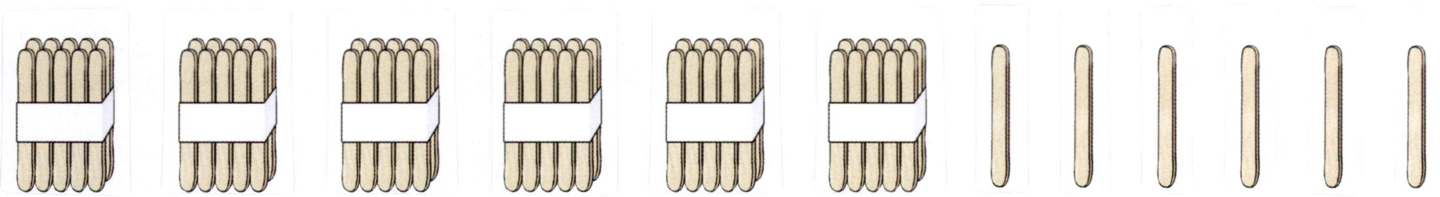

Sticker Set 10
Use on page 53 (**Unit 2**).

Test 1 Study Page • Review

Remove, answer and glue in your notebook.

Unit 1: Patterns and Equalities

1. Color the ◯ using the patterns.

a. pattern ▶ 2 (orange) and 2 (yellow)

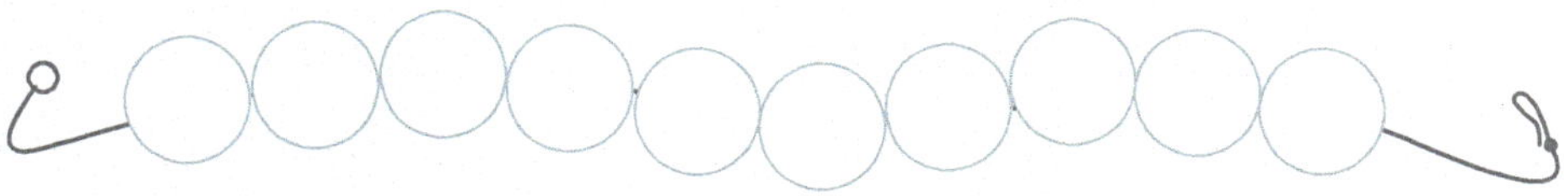

b. pattern ▶ 1 (blue), 1 (green) and 2 (orange)

2. Identify the patterns and continue the sequences.

a. 14 ➡ 17 ➡ 20 ➡ ☐ ➡ ☐

b. 0 ➡ 9 ➡ 18 ➡ ☐ ➡ ☐

c. 45 ➡ 40 ➡ 35 ➡ ☐ ➡ ☐

Name: ____________________ Grade: __________

Patterns

Repetitive Patterns

pattern

Patterns and Number Sequences

+ 4 → pattern

0	4	8	12	16

number sequence

Equalities and Inequalities

Equality =

$8 + 6 = 14$

Inequality

8 does not equal 14

Test 1 Study Page • Summary

Unit 1: Patterns and Equalities

3. Draw more  or cross out the  to make equalities.

a.

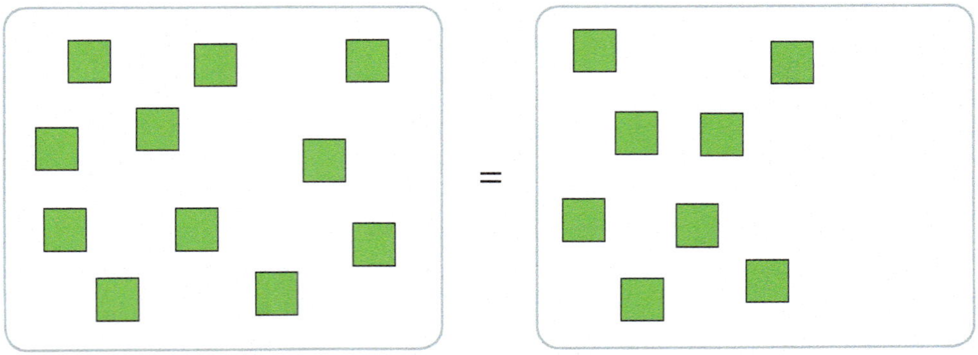

b.

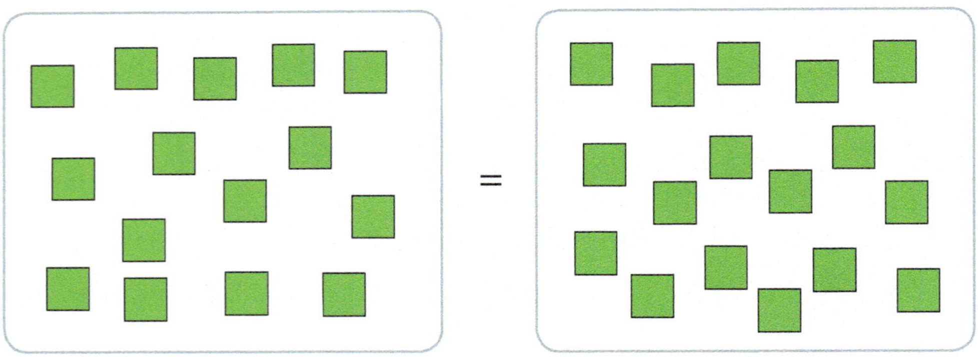

4. Write the numbers that balance the scales.

a.

b.

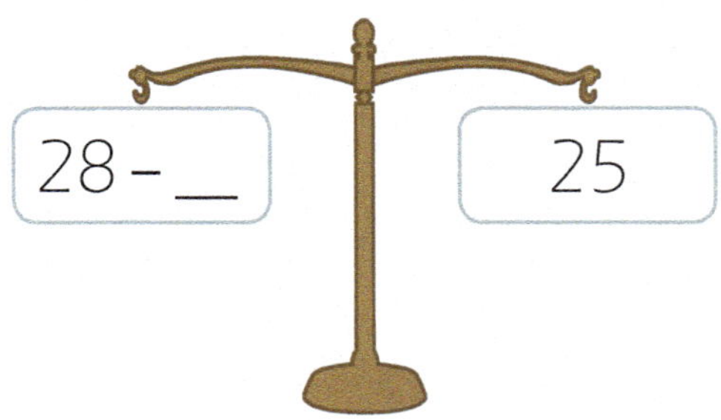

Test 2 Study Page • Review

Unit 2: Numbers Up To 100

Remove, answer and glue in your notebook.

1. Write the correct numbers of ice-cream sticks.

a.

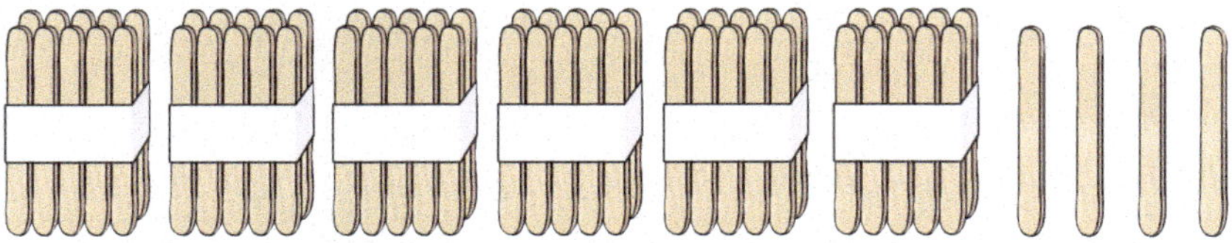

The number is ☐.

Its word form is: ______________________________.

b.

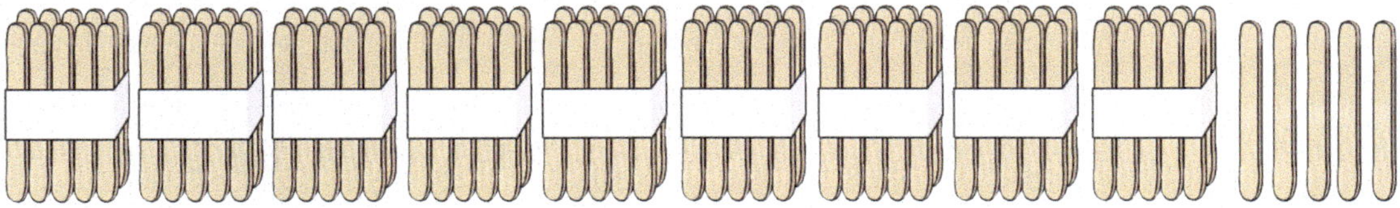

The number is ☐.

Its word form is: ______________________________.

2. Put the numbers in order.

25 56 77 65 52

a. From smallest to greatest: ☐ ☐ ☐ ☐ ☐

b. From greatest to smallest: ☐ ☐ ☐ ☐ ☐

Name: ______________________ Grade: ________

Numbers Up To 100	Ones, Tens and Hundreds	182 = 1 hundred, 8 tens and 2 ones H T O
	Reading and Writing	43 is 40 + 3 forty-three
	Place Value	The digit 6 represents: 60 in the number 62 6 in the number 26
	Composing and Decomposing	94 = 9 T and 4 O 90 + 4
Comparing and Putting Numbers in Order	Comparing and Putting in Order	58 is greater than 42 50 + 8 40 + 2 50 is greater than 40
	Estimating Quantities	An estimate of 10 muffins fit on the tray. 
Math Strategies	Math Strategies	• Counting from one addend • Counting backward • Using a numbered tape

Test 2 Study Page • Summary

Unit 2: Numbers Up To 100

3. Estimate using the referent.

There are 15 marbles.

How many marbles do you need to fill the jar? ______________________

4. Write the number of tens and ones.

a. 28 ➡ ______ T and ______ O

b. 30 ➡ ______ T and ______ O

c. 5 ➡ ______ T and ______ O

5. Decompose the numbers.

a. 65 = ______ T + ______ O

b. 79 = ______ T + ______ O

6. Draw the jumps on the numbered tape and then write the answers.

a. 23 + 22 = ☐

22	23	…	33	…	43	44	45	46	47

b. 26 − 14 = ☐

27	26	…	16	15	14	13	12	11	10

Test 3 Study Page • Review

Unit 3: Measurement, Geometry and Data

Remove, answer and glue in your notebook.

1. Mark the date on the calendar.

M	T	W	Th	F	Sa	S
						1
2	3	4	5	6	7	8
9	10	11	12	13	14	15
16	17	18	19	20	21	22
23	24	25	26	27	28	29
30						

2. Measure the objects with your hand.

a. Length of your pencil case: ☐ hands.

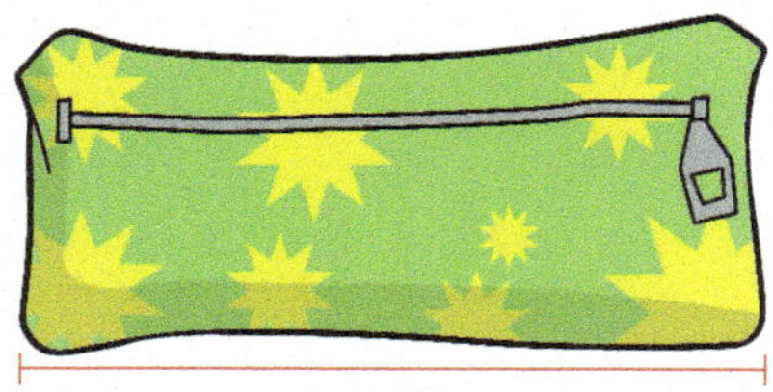

b. Width of your math notebook: ☐ hands.

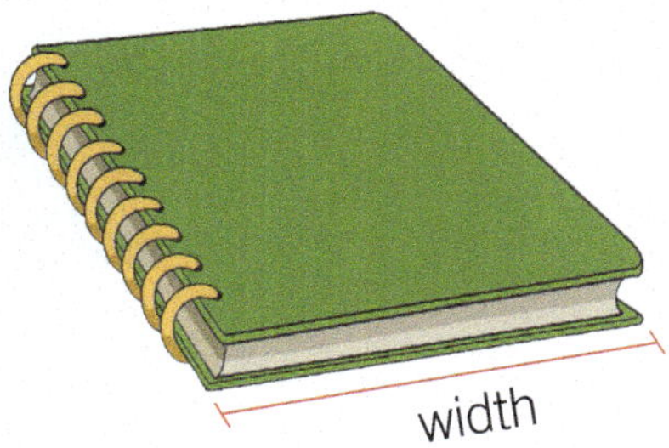

Name: ______________________________ Grade: __________

Location, Time and Measurement

Location

Prepositions can describe where things are: on, under, behind, in front of, left, right.

Time

You can use a calendar to organize your time.

Measuring With Your Body and Objects

You can use non-standardized units, such as your hand or a pencil, to measure things.

Two-Dimensional Shapes

Two-Dimensional Shapes

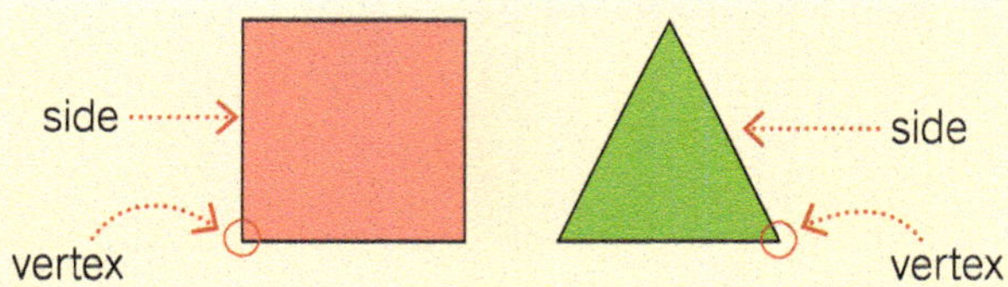

Data

Collecting and Interpreting Data

Tables help you organize and understand data.

Number of Points Scored		
Name	**Tally**	**Total**
John	||||||	6
Mike	||||	4

Recording Data in Block Charts

Block charts help you record data. They are colored according to the number of elements in each category.

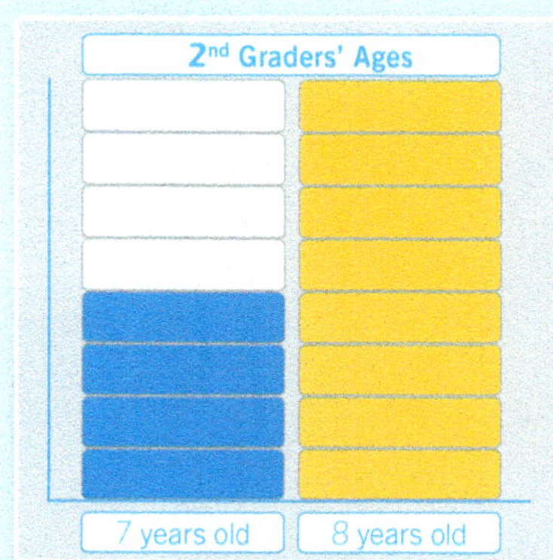

Test 3 Study Page • Summary

Unit 3: Measurement, Geometry and Data

3. Color the sides in  and the vertices in  .

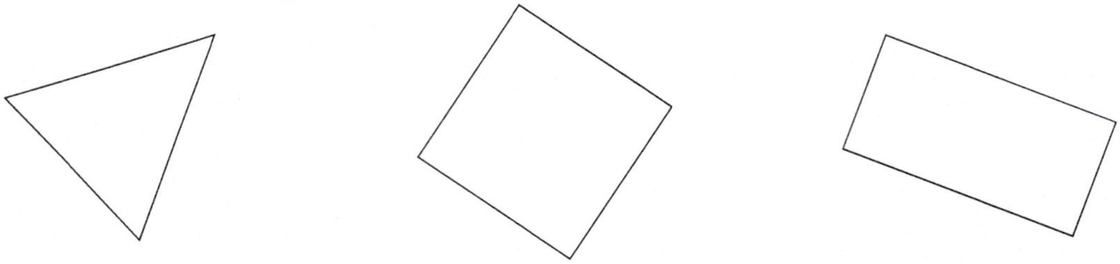

4. Do the activity.

A survey asked 10 students to choose their favorite sport. Here are the results:

basketball, soccer, swimming, basketball, swimming, soccer, basketball, soccer, basketball, soccer

a. Complete the table with the information above.

Favorite Sport		
Sport	**Tally**	**Total**
Soccer		
Swimming		
Basketball		

b. Complete the block chart with the information above.

glue here

glue here

glue here

glue here

glue here

Test 4 Study Page • Review

Remove, answer and glue in your notebook.

Unit 4: Numbers and Operations Up To 1,000

1. Complete the table.

a. 

b. 

	Number	Word Form
a.		
b.		

2. Order the numbers from smallest to greatest.

432, 347, 844, 485, 381, 836

___, ___, ___, ___, ___, ___

3. Compose and decompose the numbers.

a. 900 + 10 + 3 = ___

b. 402 = ___ + ___ + ___

Name: ______________________________ Grade: __________

Numbers Up To 1,000

Reading and Writing Numbers Up To 1,000	584 is written five hundred eighty-four
Counting by Hundreds	Count forward by 100s 328 428 528 628
Hundreds and Thousands	10 hundreds equal 1 thousand 10 H = 1 Th
Place Value	The digit 3 has different values: • 300 in the number 321 • 30 in the number 132 • 3 in the number 213
Composing and Decomposing Numbers	Composing ▶ $400 + 10 + 8 = 418$ Decomposing ▶ $793 = 700 + 90 + 3$

Addition and Subtraction

Addition and Subtraction Strategies	$845 = 800 \quad 40 \quad 5$ $-231 = 200 \quad 30 \quad 1$ $600 + 10 + 4 = 614$
Word Problems with Addition and Subtraction	**1.** Read the word problem. **2.** Identify the information that answers the question. **3.** Choose the correct operation. **4.** Choose a strategy to solve the problem.

Test 4 Study Page • Summary

Unit 4: Numbers and Operations Up To 1,000

4. Solve the operations.

a.

	H	T	O
	2	6	0
+	2	1	0

260 = ☐ ☐ ☐
+210 = ☐ ☐ ☐
☐ + ☐ + ☐ = ☐

b.

	H	T	O
	7	8	9
−	3	1	3

789 = ☐ ☐ ☐
− 313 = ☐ ☐ ☐
☐ + ☐ + ☐ = ☐

5. Solve the word problem.

There are 674 people in a theater. 362 are children and the rest are adults. How many adults are in the theater?

information ▸ ____________________

____

☐ addition
☐ subtraction

strategy

answer ▸ ____________________

glue here
glue here
glue here
glue here
glue here

Test 5 Study Page • Review

Unit 5: Multiplication and Number Sequences

Remove, answer and glue in your notebook.

1. Complete the number sequences.

a. Count by 2s. Start at 20 and count backward.

20, 18, 16, 14, ____, ____

b. Count by 5s. Start at 35 and count forward.

35, 40, 45, 50, ____, ____

c. Count by 10s. Start at 100 and count backward.

100, 90, 80, 70, ____, ____

2. Use the pictures to complete the sentences.

a.

There are ____ boxes.

Each box has ____ eggs.

There are ____ times ____ eggs.

b.

There are ____ flower vases.

Each flower vase has ____ flowers.

There are ____ times ____ flowers.

Name: ______________________________ Grade: __________

Math Strategies

Counting by 2s, 5s and 10s

forward by 2s ▶ 2, 4, 6, 8, 10, …

forward by 5s ▶ 5, 10, 15, 20, 25, …

backward by 10s ▶ 100, 90, 80, 70, 60, …

Representing Multiplication

Groups with Equal Numbers of Objects

There are **2 groups**.
Each group has **3 balls**.

There are **2 times 3** balls.

Multiplication as Repeated Addition

$5 + 5 + 5 + 5$

4 **times** 5

$4 \times 5 = 20$

Number Sequences

Representing

3 2 1

Continuing

+ 2 + 2 + 2 + 2

2 → 4 → 6 → 8 → 10

Completing

+ 3 + 3 + 3 + 3

3 → 6 → 9 → 12 → 15

Test 5 Study Page • Summary

Unit 5: Multiplication and Number Sequences

3. Write and represent the multiplication using ●.

6 times 2

_____ × _____

4. Use addition to solve the multiplication operations.

a. 2 × 8 = ☐ + ☐ = ☐

b. 4 × 7 = ☐ + ☐ + ☐ + ☐ = ☐

5. Use the patterns to continue and complete the number sequences.

a. −5 −5 −5 −5 −5 −5 −5

85	80	75					

b. +6 +6 +6 +6 +6 +6 +6

26	32			50			

c. +7 +7 +7 +7 +7 +7 +7

48			69			90	

glue here
glue here
glue here
glue here
glue here